"In this book, Sherrie M. Vavrichek skillful ioral therapy, Buddhist psychology and philosophy, and her own insight. The compassionate assertiveness approach offers powerful tools to grow beyond conflict strategies that no longer serve, without doing violence to oneself or others. Her book is a valuable contribution that will be a great help to many."

—Sharon Salzberg, author of *Real Happiness*

"It's (relatively) straightforward to be simply compassionate; the same goes for being assertive. But being both at the same time is a real challenge, even though that's the sweet spot in significant relationships of any kind. Sherrie M. Vavrichek has done a remarkable job in offering heartfelt, solid, down-to-earth, and effective ways to occupy this sweet spot at home and work."

—Rick Hanson, PhD, author of *Buddha's Brain*

"In her accessible and deeply wise book, Sherrie M. Vavrichek teaches us how to communicate our truths in a way that serves understanding and connection. The mindfulness and skills at the center of this training can transform and heal not only individual relationships, but the fabric of our society."

—Tara Brach, PhD, clinical psychologist, meditation teacher and author of *Radical Acceptance* and *True Refuge*

"Well-written, thoughtful, and incredibly enlightening. This book adeptly weaves philosophy and psychology into an interpersonal approach that can have a major positive impact on anyone's life."

—Jon E. Grant, MD, professor of psychiatry at the University of Minnesota and author of *Stop Me Because I Can't Stop Myself*

"As someone brought up on traditional assertiveness training, I have to say that Sherrie M. Vavrichek's book brings a newer, much better and more usable approach to helping people with problems in this area. It is a thoughtful, well-written gem, and a genuine resource. I can truly see myself recommending this to my own patients."

—Fred Penzel, PhD, author of *Obsessive-Compulsive Disorders* and *The Hair-Pulling Problem*

"*The Guide to Compassionate Assertiveness* is a joyously practical marriage of Western psychotherapy and Eastern wisdom. Clearly written with many helpful examples, it presents valuable skills that sensitive people need in dealing with the world."

—Kate Berg, PhD, geneticist, writer and yoga instructor at Quiet Willow Studio in Silver Spring, MD

"As a therapist/healer I found Vavrichek's book inspiring. This unique approach of blending Buddhist principles and cognitive behavioral strategies provides a useful and practical guide on how to navigate through your life assertively in a gentler and truly loving way."

—Merrill Black, LCSW, Reiki master and hypnotherapist specializing in anxiety disorders

"Drawing on her experiences with Eastern and Western philosophies, Vavrichek has created a unique approach that combines humanism with self-empowerment. If you are looking to apply assertiveness skills in all major areas of your life, then you owe it to yourself to read the wisdom in this life-affirming book."

—Joel F. Jaro, LCSW-R, psychotherapist and inspirational coach

"In this book, Vavrichek has combined the classic cognitive behavioral technique of assertiveness training with age-old philosophical principles of compassion, mindfulness and kindness. In doing so she provides a framework for assertiveness for the new millennium—effective, constructive and caring. Her writing is clear, convincing, and filled with many illuminating case examples. The author's expertise and compassion shine through as she leads the reader on a valuable journey of the mind and heart. There is wisdom in this book from which all readers will benefit."

> —Charles S. Mansueto, PhD, director at Behavior Therapy Center of Greater Washington

"Ms. Vavrichek tackles the complexities of human thinking, emotions, and interactions, while presenting her writing using style and language that are accessible to the general reader. She guides us toward reaching our ability to remain calm and caring while at the same time taking care of ourselves, without making excuses for others or allowing mistreatment. Sherrie M. Vavrichek accomplishes an amazing task, which is to integrate a Western psychological approach with Eastern Buddhist principles. She presents a new view of assertiveness: when you behave assertively with a caring heart, you are actually showing concern not just for your own, but for the other person's welfare."

> —Noah Weintraub, PsyD, clinical psychologist at Behavior Therapy Center of Greater Washington

"Using language elegant in its ease of delivery, Sherrie M. Vavrichek's groundbreaking book clearly outlines how utilizing assertiveness from a truly compassionate stance has the ability to transform problematic human communications for the better. I would say in many ways this book provides the missing link for the Western mind's step-by-step understanding of how one can develop socially conscious, healthy, interpersonal engagement skills, while simultaneously getting one's needs met! My own well-being has unexpectedly improved since reading this important work, and I suggest this approach be taught as soon as a human being is developmentally able to grasp these concepts. Much unnecessary suffering would be eliminated."

— Christina Pearson, founding director at Trichotillomania Learning Center in Santa Cruz, CA

"A true gem: A thoughtful, cohesive, and comprehensive work that spans scientific research, Eastern and Western concepts and application, distilling information into an engaging, readable, and practical book that many can benefit from. Sherrie M. Vavrichek has provided a roadmap that guides the reader through chartered and unchartered waters. She shows the reader a way to be assertive while also caring, even in the most complex and demanding of situations. A quietly powerful, impactful book."

— Sarah Weden, PsyD, neuropsychologist at NeuroBehavioral Associates in Columbia, MD

The guide to
COMPASSIONATE
ASSERTIVENESS

How to Express Your Needs
& Deal with Conflict While
Keeping a Kind Heart

SHERRIE M. VAVRICHEK, LCSW-C

NEW HARBINGER PUBLICATIONS, INC.

Publisher's Note

This publication is designed to provide accurate and authoritative information in regard to the subject matter covered. It is sold with the understanding that the publisher is not engaged in rendering psychological, financial, legal, or other professional services. If expert assistance or counseling is needed, the services of a competent professional should be sought.

Distributed in Canada by Raincoast Books

Copyright © 2012 by Sherrie Mansfield Vavrichek
New Harbinger Publications, Inc.
5674 Shattuck Avenue
Oakland, CA 94609
www.newharbinger.com

Acquired by Tesilya Hanauer; Cover design by Amy Shoup;
Edited by Rosalie Wieder; Text design by Tracy Carlson

Library of Congress Cataloging-in-Publication Data

Vavrichek, Sherrie Mansfield.
  The guide to compassionate assertiveness : how to express your needs and deal with conflict while keeping a kind heart / Sherrie M. Vavrichek.
    p. cm.
  Includes bibliographical references.
  ISBN 978-1-60882-171-6 (pbk. : alk. paper) -- ISBN 978-1-60882-172-3 (pdf e-book) -- ISBN 978-1-60882-173-0 (epub)
  1. Assertiveness (Psychology) 2. Interpersonal communication. I. Title.
  BF575.A85V38 2012
  158.2--dc23

                        2012011780

Printed in the United States of America

14 13 12   10 9 8 7 6 5 4 3 2 1   First printing

This book is dedicated to my family, with love.

Contents

PART 1

Learning about Yourself and How Compassionate Assertiveness Can Help You

CHAPTER 1

Exploring Your Interpersonal Style and How You Became the Person You Are

CHAPTER 2

Compassionate Assertiveness: Improving Communication and Solving Problems with an Open Heart

PART 2

Training Your Mind and Your Heart

PART 3

Strengthening Your Interpersonal Skills

Acknowledgments

This book could not have been created without the goodwill, generosity, and expert knowledge of the many people who have supported and helped me over the years in both my personal and my professional life.

To my mother, Gertrude, my first and most important role model, who taught me right from wrong, and who has guided me with her love, humor, and wisdom, and to my father, Robert, who encouraged me to work hard, be creative, and live life to its fullest, I offer my deepest gratitude. I also offer my heartfelt thanks to my grandparents, Ben, Blanche, Eddie, and Goldie, who gave me a strong foundation of love and security in my early years and beyond, which gave me the optimism to pursue my dreams. I also am very thankful to my stepfather, John, who willingly took on an "instant family" and who instilled in me a love of reading; and to my step-mother, Evelyn, and mother-in-law, Louise, who have inspired me with their strength of character and generosity and who taught me that you can learn from great role models, even as an adult. I also want to express my appreciation to my beloved brothers, Michael and Glenn, for their caring presence in my life and for their trust and faith in me, all of which gave me the confidence to follow my own path.

My husband and best friend, Bruce, has been unflagging in his patience and ongoing support of this project and has given me invaluable feedback and advice. And my daughters, Diane and Julie, who are shining lights in my life, offered me priceless advice throughout the writing process on what worked and what needed to be changed. Without these three individuals I never could have made this project a reality, and for that I offer them my deepest thanks.

On the professional side, much of what I share in this book I have learned from those who have come to me for help over the years for a variety of difficulties. Their strength, their courage, and their trust in our work have inspired me to continuously search for more effective ways to help them with their struggles so that they can live fuller, richer lives.

In addition, I have learned a great deal from many of the master teachers in the field of cognitive behavioral psychology and from the Buddhist and mindfulness meditation traditions, through direct training and by reading. Their work is cited throughout this book and in the Resources and References sections.

I would also like to acknowledge the encouragement, excellent advice, and continuous learning opportunities I have received at the Behavior Therapy Center of Greater Washington from my mentor and good friend Charles Mansueto, its director. I am most grateful, as well, to my coworkers there, especially Noah Weintraub, Dave Keuler, Ruth Golomb, and Brad Hufford, who gave me excellent pointers and suggestions about how to develop the concept of compassionate assertiveness. In addition, many thanks to Sarah Weden, Kate Berg, Jocelyn Lindsay, Betty Whitney, and Merrill Black, who generously enriched this book with their unique insights. I would also like to convey my appreciation to my dear friend Carrie Burmaster, who reignited my interest in the world of meditation several years ago, which planted the seeds for this book.

The Guide to Compassionate Assertiveness has been nurtured throughout its development by my wonderful editors at New Harbinger: Angela Autry Gorden, Tesilya Hanauer, and Rosalie Wieder, and by Will DeRooy, my outstanding proofreader. I owe a great debt to them and to other members of the New Harbinger team, including Julie Bennett, Nicola Skidmore, Heather Garnos, and Jess Beebe, for their trust in the book's value and for their expert guidance in bringing this project to fruition. Finally, many thanks to Amy Shoup, Tracy Carlson, Janice Fitch, and Michele Waters for capturing the essence of compassionate assertiveness through the creation of the book's beautiful cover and interior design.

Introduction

If you are uncomfortable asserting yourself in certain situations, you are not alone. As a clinical social worker and cognitive behavioral therapist with many years of experience, I have known hundreds of individuals who have difficulty in this area. And assertiveness problems are not just limited to a few people; many—maybe even all—of us have struggled with assertiveness problems from time to time. Perhaps, like some people, you acquiesce when you are asked to do something you don't want to do, for fear of hurting someone's feelings or because you are afraid someone will be angry or disappointed. Perhaps you don't voice your opinion because you are worried that others will criticize you, or you hold back from making reasonable requests for fear of being turned down. Or you might hold back from expressing your feelings (including positive feelings) because you are unsure about how the other person will respond. Or it is possible that you do not address problems because you are afraid that you might lose your temper and say or do something you might regret.

The people who come to me for help with assertiveness are generally very kind and sensitive individuals who hold back from talking about their feelings or concerns. Unfortunately, they sometimes pay a high price for their reluctance to speak up. They may harbor silent resentments or hold back until they just can't take it anymore, at which point they "blow up, fall apart, or end relationships." Far too often these individuals find themselves being taken advantage of or put in uncomfortable situations where they feel frustrated, fearful, angry, or unappreciated; and they often suffer greatly from feelings of unworthiness, confusion, or anger toward themselves or others.

For years I used a standard cognitive behavioral method called "assertiveness training" with people who had these kinds of assertiveness problems. This approach emphasizes standing up for your equality and rights using cool, direct, firm, and persistent techniques. However, while assertiveness training was helpful for some people, many others felt that the "cure" was worse than the "disease." Some felt this way because of their anxiety over how others might respond to the firm and cool approach that assertiveness training encourages. Others who resisted the assertiveness training approach were people who struggled with low self-esteem and did not have the energy or confidence to go head-to-head with others in the way that this approach proposes. Then, too, there were people who had what might be called "social scrupulosity," a term I use for those with excessive concern about hurting the feelings of others. These people feel that a direct approach that emphasizes their own needs would be unnecessarily upsetting or hurtful to others. But many of the people who were not comfortable with assertiveness training techniques simply valued kindness and generosity very highly, either because of the way they were brought up or because their own personal journey had led them to emphasize the welfare of others, and they therefore believed that addressing concerns should be done in a very caring way.

Moreover, many books on assertiveness training struck me and other therapists I know as being problematic because they neglected the importance of having concern for the benefit of others, as well as oneself. My interest in helping people become more assertive while also validating their caring interpersonal styles and values led me to conclude that some other approach was needed, but I wasn't sure what.

I found a way to address this dilemma in my practice somewhat by chance, when my interest in the Eastern practices of yoga and meditation, which I had first explored when I was in my twenties, was renewed. Now, years later, I again saw how these practices, including Buddhist-based mindfulness and meditation, helped me feel physically and mentally stronger and gave me a more flexible and calmer way to respond to stressful situations. As these practices enriched my own life, I became increasingly convinced that including this philosophical perspective in my work as a cognitive behavioral therapist could be very helpful to those who came to me for help with a variety of difficulties, including nonassertiveness.

Meanwhile, I had also seen how over the years the field of psychology had begun to change. Softer versions of assertiveness training had become available (for example, Paterson 2000). Mindfulness had found a place in newer forms of cognitive behavioral psychology, including positive psychology, dialectical behavior therapy, and acceptance and commitment therapy (Hayes et al. 2011), and a more caring attitude had been incorporated into the fields of communication and negotiation (McKay, Davis, and Fanning 2009). I came to realize that I could integrate aspects of communication literature, cognitive behavioral psychology, and Buddhist philosophy to create something useful for the general public as well as for people who were especially anxious or sensitive. I called this integrated approach "compassionate assertiveness," and sharing it with you is the reason that I wrote this book. My main primary sources are Buddhism and cognitive behavioral therapy. However, since the concepts in the compassionate assertiveness approach are found in many other religious, literary, and philosophic teachings, I will at times also quote or refer to other sources in order to honor the universality of these messages.

In the following chapters you will find the results of several years of refining the theory, practice, and application of compassionate assertiveness. And it is my sincere hope that, just as this method has helped others, it will enrich your life and strengthen your relationships.

The Structure of This Book

In the pages that follow, you will find a step-by-step approach to expanding your perspective and honing your interpersonal skills, with a special focus on learning how to assert yourself in a caring and confident way. The book is divided into four parts. In part 1 you will learn more about your own unique interactive tendencies, strengths, and vulnerabilities, along with the foundation and components of compassionate assertiveness.

In part 2 you will look inward, the first step to cultivating more mutually respectful and caring relationships. The chapters in this section include ways to cultivate the compassionate assertiveness tools of gratitude, equanimity, courage, and forgiveness.

Part 3 will introduce you to calming and mindfulness exercises, active listening and communication techniques, and effective ways to negotiate and solve problems. Together with the material presented in the previous section, these chapters will complete your compassionate assertiveness "tool kit." Part 4 will show you how to apply the steps of compassionate assertiveness to the specific challenges you might encounter with your partner, with your family, and in the outside world.

How to Benefit from This Book

You might want to try reading this book quickly all the way through to get an overview of the general approach, marking the passages that feel most relevant to you. Then read the book again more slowly, allowing yourself time to contemplate the ideas and apply them to your life.

Throughout the book you will find exercises that invite you to practice the concepts being presented. I strongly encourage you to try them so that you can tailor compassionate assertiveness to your own unique set of circumstances and get the greatest benefit from this approach. Like the help you would need if you were to go on a challenging journey such as trekking in a mountain range, think of this book as a guide that will provide you with a map and tools to help you toward success. Trust that if you are dedicated to this process, you can begin to dissolve fear, anger, and resentment, and will be better able to interact with others in an effective and caring manner. My hope for you is that by the end of the book you will be well on your way on this important interpersonal journey—that you will grow stronger with each step along the way and that your burdens will grow lighter with each new day.

PART 1

Learning about Yourself and How Compassionate Assertiveness Can Help You

CHAPTER 1

Exploring Your Interpersonal Style and How You Became the Person You Are

Given that you are reading this book, you probably have some concerns about yourself (or someone you know) with regard to assertiveness. Perhaps you have a hard time speaking up or entering into conversations. Maybe it's hard for you to set limits or to ask others for help. Or perhaps it's hard for you to talk about your feelings, whether positive or negative. What holds you back? One barrier for many people is that they aren't sure how to reach out or speak up in a confident yet caring way. This happens to most of us from time to time, but if it is a frequent problem for you, learning more about yourself may help you both work with your difficulties and capitalize on your strengths.

In this chapter, you will learn about your unique interpersonal style, including both its positive and its problematic aspects. You will also explore some of the influences in your life and contemplate how they have affected how you think about yourself and others.

The following quiz describes some interpersonal situations that might be difficult for you. Taking it will help you learn about your interpersonal style and will also lay the groundwork for reading the chapters that follow. So sharpen your pencil and let's get started.

An Invitation: Discover Your Interpersonal Style

1. *You go to a party where you see a new person who is getting a lot of attention from your friends. You feel a little left out and ignored. You:*

   A. *Go over to the group and join in the conversation*

   B. *Sit alone for a while and consider leaving the party*

   C. *Wander around the house a bit, looking at the host's bookshelves*

2. *Your partner says he wants to go camping together for the weekend. You don't really want to go camping, but you worry that he'll be angry if you say you'd rather do something else. You:*

   A. *Think about a way that you can work in a side trip to somewhere that you would like to go*

   B. *Feel annoyed and hope he notices your lack of interest*

   C. *Say it's okay but find yourself delaying getting ready*

3. *A friend asks your opinion about an opportunity that she has. You feel a little envious about it. You are most likely to:*

   A. *Wonder if there are ways that you could be included*

   B. *Think of many of the downsides*

   C. *Feel very curious and want to ask a lot of questions*

4. *A relative asks to borrow something from you. You don't really want to lend it because it is fragile and valuable. You are most likely to:*

   A. *Meet his request graciously and hope for the best*

   B. *Reluctantly agree to make the loan but feel irritated and put on the spot*

   C. *Agree to loan the item and not let yourself think about your discomfort*

5. *A telephone solicitor calls. You don't really need the item, but she makes it sound like a really good deal and you are uncomfortable saying no. You make the purchase and:*

    A. *Figure that you'll probably like it*

    B. *Are angry with yourself and with the telephone solicitor*

    C. *Put it out of your mind*

6. *A subordinate at work writes a report that could use a little editing. You:*

    A. *Correct it yourself*

    B. *Point out the errors but feel worried that she'll be upset*

    C. *Leave the report as is, since the edits would have been very small*

7. *Another person gets waited on at the sales counter even though you think that you were there first. You don't say anything. You:*

    A. *Look around to see if there is something else to purchase*

    B. *Are upset with the sales clerk and the other customer*

    C. *Don't feel too upset because you are not positive you were there first*

8. *You are shopping at a mall with a friend. You don't have a lot of extra money to spend and don't really need anything. After an hour you would like to leave. You are most likely to:*

    A. *Look for something to buy that's marked way down so you can then end the shopping trip*

    B. *Feel annoyed and start to resent the other person's insensitivity to you*

    C. *Go along with the situation but start daydreaming*

9. *People who know you well are most likely to say that some of your greatest strengths are:*

A. *How gracious and enthusiastic you are*

B. *Your intelligence, competence, and honesty*

C. *Your nonjudgmental attitude, laid-back manner, and amiability*

10. *In your heart, something that bothers you about yourself is your tendency toward:*

A. *Dissatisfaction with what you have or wanting to have your own way*

B. *Anger or the tendency to avoid people you aren't getting along with*

C. *Confusion or inattentiveness that creates problems in your relationships*

The three choices noted for each item in the preceding quiz illustrate problems with assertiveness that reflect three basic interpersonal styles: *enthusiastic (A), discerning (B), and open-minded (C)*. If you add up the number of times you chose each letter, you might notice that one style dominates. However, there may be a tie for first place, an obvious secondary style, or a three-way tie. There is no right or wrong, or better or worse profile. Whatever your scores are, your type is just a conceptual label for you to keep in mind as you move through the book.

In the following pages, you will learn about these three different interpersonal styles, as well as the different causes and conditions in your life that may have contributed to the way that you relate to others. At the end of this chapter, and each of the following ones, you will find a box that addresses ways you can apply the lessons in the chapter to your specific interpersonal style(s). In this way, you will be able to tailor your efforts to meet your unique needs.

Taking a Look at Your Interpersonal Style

This section provides a detailed description of each of the three interpersonal styles: enthusiastic, discerning, and open-minded. But before we proceed, you might want to know how the typology used here was developed. Actually, it is based on a system that was developed about 1,600 years ago by a Buddhist scholar in order to help monks determine the kind of meditation they would find most useful. It initially used categories consisting of three pairs of negative/positive traits, translated as follows: *greedy/dedicated*, characterized by craving/optimism; *aversive/discerning wisdom*, characterized by criticism/clarity; and *deluded/open-minded*, characterized by doubt/equanimity (Schmidt 2009). Over the centuries the concept of temperament types has evolved, been elaborated upon, and been adapted to modern-day concerns (Kornfield 2008). Although it is in your best interest to cultivate the positive qualities and make efforts to manage the problematic aspects of all three groups, it may be helpful for you to focus on your most prominent individual interpersonal style(s) and how it relates to your ability to interact with others in a positive way in day-to-day life. As you read about each style, I encourage you to begin to think about ways to cultivate your unique strengths and to work on your areas of difficulty.

A. The Enthusiastic Interpersonal Style

I think of the enthusiastic interpersonal style as the one that most closely represents the heart. A person with an enthusiastic interpersonal style is usually optimistic, with faith in the world. He or she is often a creative person who loves beauty and the bountiful pleasures that life has to offer. If the majority of your answers were A's, you probably know how to have fun, are a faithful friend, and make every effort to be sure that those around you are happy and comfortable. You relish ideas and experiences as well, and you enjoy planning events and vacations and reminiscing about them afterward. You are generous, enthusiastic, and charitable, and you offer encouragement and support to others.

Your enthusiasm can be thought of as a kind of emotional energy that involves an attraction toward experiences, people, and things. In its highest form, your desire for the good things in life and your concern for others have a spacious and graceful quality. At your best you exemplify one of Buddhism's fundamental virtues: *loving-kindness*, or the wish for happiness for yourself and for others as well.

The challenging aspects of the enthusiastic interpersonal style. Sounds great? It turns out that too much of a good thing can cause it to turn sour, and that includes enthusiasm. While there are many positive aspects to having an enthusiastic style, if your attractions become too strong they can reveal a tendency toward grasping and desiring things too much. Grasping can hold the seductive illusion that you will be happier if you can just get or do that one more or better thing, and this can create an unhealthy ambition or a sense of rivalry or jealousy toward others. Grasping can relate to material objects (such as yearning for a fancy car), social status (wanting that prestigious job), or even relationships (wishing that your spouse could be as charming as your friend's). It can also reinforce tendencies toward egotism and narcissism—the feeling that you are more special and better than others.

When this happens, grasping can lead to suffering because of the "hungry" energy that is fueled by the belief that you have to have what you desire. Like an addiction, this hunger can consume you, cutting you off from others and making you feel impatient and restless. And just as a fire is in constant need of being stoked, grasping for what you desire can rob you of the ability to be content with your life as it is (Chodron 2007).

Finding the balance. If you have an enthusiastic interpersonal style, you have many qualities that draw people to you, but be aware that certain grasping tendencies can work against you. Your ability to understand and work with the difference between healthy attraction to desirable things on one hand, and greed or clinging on the other, will help your interpersonal interactions and relationships flourish. For instance, if you tend to be insistent or use manipulation to get your way, you can remind yourself that whatever you are grasping for is impermanent, a "mixed bag" of good and bad, and in the long run not as important to your happiness as you may think. This perspective will help you keep your enthusiasm but also know when to let go.

An Invitation: Contemplate Your Enthusiastic Interpersonal Tendencies

Think about one or two of your relationships. Are there times when grasping or clinging to your desires backfires on you? On occasion are you evasive so that you can get what you want? Ask yourself if you might be willing to soften your desires for things to be a certain way for the sake of your relationships with others.

Now, bring to your awareness the positive and priceless aspects of being enthusiastic and caring—the happy times that you have had with others, your acts of generosity and kindness, and the enjoyment of life that you share with those around you. When you are aware of your positive energy and of its many benefits to you and to others, you have come home to your own true nature.

B. The Discerning Interpersonal Style

The discerning interpersonal style is the one that I think of as most closely associated with intellect or the mind. Someone with a discerning interpersonal style has clarity of thought, strength of conviction, integrity, honesty, discipline, and a strong sense of responsibility. If you have these tendencies you have the courage to stand up for what you think is right, are highly motivated to find solutions to problems, and are willing to take the time and effort to do so. You often display a sharp and self-deprecating sense of humor, which at times can charm people with its disarming honesty. You are most likely one of the hardest workers in your workplace, and your supervisor may often turn to you when high-quality work is essential. People with discerning interpersonal tendencies are the people I would want for my doctor, accountant, or lawyer, and I imagine that you probably feel the same way. With these outstanding qualities, when you are at your best you exemplify a second fundamental Buddhist virtue: *wisdom*, the ability to see things as they really are.

The challenging aspects of the discerning interpersonal style. Your sharp mind and concern about doing what is right are unquestionably valuable qualities to have. However, the problematic side of your discerning tendencies is your potential for focusing too much on your own faults or those of others. While the enthusiastic person's major concern may be grasping at what he or she likes, yours may be a tendency to reject or try to escape from people (or experiences) you don't like. With an ever-watchful eye for finding and solving problems, you may be inclined to feel excessively critical, judgmental, or suspicious toward others.

The negative aspects of this interpersonal style can make it hard for you to connect with people in a nonjudgmental way. For instance, in your attempts to meet very high standards, you may find it hard to relax and enjoy the company of others. Furthermore, you might even find yourself resenting those who have fun because you may not allow this for yourself. An extreme of the problematic aspect of this interpersonal style is when you feel hatred or contempt toward yourself or others for not meeting your high standards—at that point you have lost track of what is really important and positive in your life.

Finding the balance. As someone with discerning tendencies, you can build on your undeniable strengths while softening the sharp edges of your critical inclinations. Because you have such strength of character and courage, you can train yourself to be patient and kind toward others as well as toward yourself. With your exceptional intelligence you can challenge your need to be right and can look at the cost of needlessly correcting others. And you can use your integrity and honesty to allow yourself to be vulnerable, to ask for help when you need it, and to trust that if you throw in a good dose of appreciation for what others have to offer they will be more receptive to your ideas. Finally, as you begin to realize that you don't have to be perfect in order to be loved (and that, in fact, human perfection is not even possible), you can extend that same attitude of acceptance toward others.

An Invitation: Contemplate Your Discerning Interpersonal Tendencies

Think about one or two of your relationships. Are you at times overly critical or judgmental? Can you consider that maybe the judging you are doing is causing your relationships to suffer? Is it possible that there are times when arguing to make a point backfires on you? Ask yourself if you might be willing to allow yourself to let go of some of your negativity for the sake of your relationships, even if it is uncomfortable to do so.

Now, bring to your awareness the wonderfully positive aspects of being in the discerning group—the strength, intelligence, honesty, reliability, and strong sense of commitment to excellence. Honor your integrity and your courage. Believe that you can distance yourself from your anger and use your strengths to connect with others in a constructive and caring way. When you are in that place of positive energy, you have come home to your own true nature, and your reward will be the love, respect, and appreciation that you have been longing for.

C. The Open-Minded Interpersonal Style

I think of the open-minded interpersonal style as the one that most closely reflects the spirit. If you primarily use this style, you are most likely an accepting and easygoing person. You have a deep sense of fairness and balance and can see both sides of every issue. You are flexible when you go out with others, because it is the experience of being with friends that is important to you, not the details of the event. Your indifference to a lot of superficial things that may be important to other people reflects deeper values that are appreciated by others. You have the ability to accept the differences between people without judging them. There is a kind of innocence and honest vulnerability about you that is reflected in how you avoid manipulating or controlling others. At your best, you have a calm countenance and the ability to step back and look at the big picture in a dispassionate and peaceful manner.

Buddhist philosophy greatly values these qualities and encourages people to cultivate them. You naturally relate to concepts of spaciousness and balance, and your open awareness recognizes that many of the things people fret about are not important in the grand scheme of things because they are temporary or may not even come to pass. At your best, your calm and open way of relating to others exemplifies a third fundamental Buddhist virtue: *equanimity*, the ability to be at ease and to view reality with clarity and without prejudice.

The challenging aspects of the open-minded interpersonal style. Although your laid-back qualities are most admirable, your spaciousness can at times become "spacey" or lead you to have a "foggy" way of moving through life. There may be times, for instance, when you do not want to be aware of your feelings or experiences because they are difficult to face, so you ignore them. When confronted with complex issues, you may become overwhelmed and bury your head in the sand, failing to notice things that need to be done or not meeting your responsibilities in a timely fashion. If others are upset with you, you may wonder what the big deal is and dismiss their concerns as unimportant. These difficulties can lead you to alienate the people you care about and may even compromise relationships that are important to you.

When friends or relatives ask you to weigh in with an opinion, you might vacillate between different points of view and become confused and indecisive. When this happens you may decide that it doesn't matter to you, or allow yourself to be too easily swayed by the crowd. As a friend of mine once said, "It's good to be open-minded, but you don't want to be so open-minded that your brains fall out." In scenarios like these, your tendency to tune out what is happening within you or with the people around you may lead to an illusion that everything is fine when it is not.

Finding the balance. Your peaceful and accepting countenance tends to attract people because they trust you and are confident that you won't judge them; because of your open and balanced perspective, others see you as a safe harbor during stormy times. But hard as it may be, it is also important to tune in to your own feelings and needs as well as those of others and to face your own inner difficulties as well as interpersonal problems. With practice you can discipline yourself to do certain things because they are important to other people, even if they are not important to you. It may also mean showing a little more initiative at home and at work. There is no doubt that you have the capacity to build on your caring, accepting, and balanced way of dealing with the world. Trust that when your energy is channeled toward acknowledging and responding to the reality within you and around you, your clarity of vision, openheartedness, and patient manner will endear you to the people in your life.

An Invitation: Contemplate Your Open-Minded Interpersonal Tendencies

Take a moment to think about one or two of your relationships. Are you at times negligent or careless? Do you deny or ignore important matters even though there might be significant consequences? Do you assume that others will make hard decisions so you don't have to? Consider the possibility that there are times when drifting along gets in the way of your personal growth. Ask yourself if you might be willing to push yourself to really pay attention to what is present—even if it is uncomfortable to do so—for the sake of your own happiness as well as for the sake of your relationships with others.

Now bring to your awareness how valuable it is to be someone who takes in the big picture and who stays calm and steady even when there is turmoil around you. Imagine how comforting it is for others to experience the peaceful presence of your even temper and serenity when problems arise. Your open and calm approach to life will be enhanced by your attentiveness and responsiveness to your own needs as well as to the needs of those around you. And your balanced approach can be used effectively to take a firm yet caring stand when necessary. When you are in that place of positive energy, you have come home to your own true nature.

Comparing The Three Interpersonal Styles

	General Characteristics	Potential Problems	Positive Potentiality
Enthusiastic	Desire Optimism Graciousness Dedication	Greed Grasping Jealousy	Loving-kindness
Discerning	Aversion Clarity of thought Integrity Character	Anger Hatred Judging	Wisdom

Open-Minded	Dispassion Peacefulness Balance Acceptance	Confusion Ignorance Delusion	Equanimity

What Does Your Interpersonal Style Mean for You and Your Relationships?

At our best, we can all cultivate the virtues of all three interpersonal styles: loving-kindness, wisdom, and equanimity. At our worst, we all can fall prey to grasping, hatred, and delusion. Awareness of your interpersonal style(s) can be a guidepost to the work that you need to do to meet your potential.

In your relationships, you may feel a strong affinity for people who have the same interpersonal style that you do, or you may be especially hard on them because their flaws reflect your own. Alternatively, you may enjoy rich relationships with people whose interpersonal styles are different from yours, seeing them as complementary to your own, or you may judge such people negatively for not having your strengths. Try to be aware of how both similarities and differences play themselves out in your experience of others. This will help you maintain a balanced attitude toward those around you, even when you find yourself feeling irritated or even hurt by them. Learning to recognize your lovability as well as that of others, while also knowing that there is always work to be done to meet your potential, is a first big step toward being able to work out problems and concerns with the people in your life.

How You Became the Person You Are

You might wonder how it is that you have developed your particular interpersonal style or combination of styles. The assumption of this book is that we are all influenced by many causes and conditions that can come into play at any given moment of our lives, from before birth until the present moment. Some of these causes and conditions are biological, including genetic and other factors, which can "prime" us to behave in certain ways. However, our early and current social influences make their mark on us as well. In addition, we have the ability to broaden our horizons because we can think, learn, and use our power of language and conscious awareness. Being aware of all of these elements can help us make choices about the kinds of interactions and relationships we want to have. Let's look at these elements, one by one.

Biological Influences

Although we are related to "lower" animals, our biological makeup allows us to have the most complex relationships in the animal kingdom. Several aspects of our unique biology can affect the way we interact with others.

Compassion: your human heritage. Anthropologists and psychologists have long recognized that as social animals, we human beings need to attract mates, are naturally protective toward our young, and have strong feelings of attachment, empathy, and concern for others, especially members of our own "group." The ability to bond with and protect members of their own group gave early humans important survival advantages in environments where they had to cooperate with and depend on each other for survival. This most likely laid down the biological roots of compassion and kindness, and these qualities and advantages persist to this day. Human history is replete with stories about people showing compassion toward and risking their own lives for others, sometimes even for complete strangers. I'm sure you have read human-interest news stories of heroism or generosity; and for every such act reported there are hundreds more by people who quietly help others in large and small ways out of their own sense of responsibility and humanity.

Encouraging prosocial and caring human qualities is a foundational pillar of psychology, one that has gained greater importance over time. In recent decades such psychologists as Martin Seligman, the father of positive psychology, have shown that feelings of caring and of connection with others are closely linked with feelings of well-being and happiness—and that acts of loving-kindness and compassion benefit both the giver and the receiver (Seligman 2002, 43).

And this isn't something that we have to learn; it has been shown that concern for others occurs quite spontaneously, even in very young children. In one study, one-year-olds showed distress when puppets were "hurt" by other puppets (Bloom 2010). Other studies have found that toddlers help people without being prompted. In one such study, experimenters were hanging clothes on a clothesline when they "accidentally" dropped clothespins outside of their reach. The toddlers retrieved the clothespins many times, even though the experimenters did not praise them for doing so. Experiments with various other objects had the same results (Warneken and Tomasello 2006).

An Invitation: Remember the Kindness of Others

Think about a time when someone showed compassion and kindness to you. Maybe it was someone close to you—a grandparent or other relative. Maybe it was a teacher or a neighbor. Perhaps it was a stranger who helped you out in a time of vulnerability or need. Can you recall your emotional response to that experience?

Now think about a time when you showed concern for or assisted someone who needed help. Try to recapture that experience and how it felt to you. What was your emotional response to that experience? Can you allow yourself to believe that such acts as these express the goodness of your own true nature, which is always present but sometimes needs an opportunity to reveal itself?

The other side of the human coin. Even as we acknowledge that kindness is one of our evolutionary legacies, in order to truly understand ourselves, we also need to acknowledge the aggressive and avoidant sides of what it means to be human. Our early human ancestors had to compete for food, mates, territory, and other limited resources. Indeed, their very survival depended upon their ability to avoid, flee from, or react aggressively to threats.

Few day-to-day experiences in the modern world involve the physical dangers our distant ancestors faced. Even so, when interpersonal problems or concerns arise, instinctive freeze, fight, or flight mechanisms instantly prepare us for the physical exertion needed to physically protect ourselves from harm (Hanson 2009). The processes involved will be described in more detail in chapter 5. For now, suffice it to say that your biologically based vigilance and self-protective reactions to perceived threats can compete with your inborn compassion. Therefore, when you are in uncomfortable interpersonal situations, you most likely receive competing internal messages as some parts of your brain tell you to protect yourself, while other parts will encourage bonding and reconciliation.

Your brain is a learning machine. Your amazing human brain has another feature that can give you freedom of choice when you encounter interpersonal difficulties. That feature is called neuroplasticity. What this means is that your brain is able to recalibrate itself in the presence of new internal or external causes and conditions. Taking in new information, challenging old patterns of thought, experimenting with healthier competing thoughts, behaviors, and responses to the environment—all of these are capabilities that you can use throughout your entire life to transform your way of relating to the world.

This process is not always an easy one, however, because we all tend to automatically slide into familiar and automatic behaviors when confronted with various circumstances, and both our healthy and unhealthy habits have been strengthened with practice. Just as a coach or teacher who tries to help someone correct an inefficient golf stroke or poor handwriting can tell you, bad habits can be hard to alter, and the longer they have been in place the more challenging it can be to make those changes.

On the other hand, I am sure that you have heard about or known people with many problems who, with motivation and opportunity, were able to adopt healthy and productive ways of living their lives when conditions were right. Even hardened prisoners have been known to change their way of thinking and behaving when they are given the opportunity to look inward and see that they have more power to grow and change than they (and almost everyone else) gave themselves credit for (Bowen et al. 2006). Others have been able to use the power of their minds to rise above difficult circumstances (Boyce 2010). Some, like Mahatma Gandhi and

Nelson Mandela, were influenced by new experiences, people, or writings to develop inner strength and wisdom. They then used what they had learned to make the world a better place. In my own work, I have seen that when people learn more adaptive ways of thinking and interacting with others, when they develop courage and confidence, and when they practice these new behaviors repeatedly, they are able to make significant improvements in their quality of life and their relationships.

Genetics. You not only look like your mother and father, you also inherited certain emotional, social, and psychological tendencies from them. Several studies of identical twins (especially those adopted at birth and reunited as adults) have shed light on our understanding of the contribution of genetics to—among other things—interpersonal styles. Tom Bouchard of the University of Minnesota and his colleagues examined over one hundred sets of identical twins reared apart, who answered approximately ten thousand questions (1990). For each pair, the findings revealed many striking similarities in interests, habits, values, health, IQ, temperament, and interpersonal styles between them, even though they hadn't influenced or learned from each other. This supports what you have probably already noticed—that while we each have our own unique personality, genetics really do matter. So if you have a sense of humor like your father, or are an introvert like your mother, there may very well be a large genetic influence at play.

Life Experiences

Despite genetic and other biological factors, biology alone does not have to define or control your life. How you relate to others, for instance, is also influenced by your life experiences, both in the past and in the present.

The people and events in your life. Your family, neighbors, and peers have very likely influenced your beliefs, attitudes, values, and ways of interacting with others, maybe even in ways you are not aware of. Both my stepmother and mother-in-law, for instance, have had a tremendously positive influence on me, inspiring me with their childhood stories of being brought up on farms that had no modern conveniences. In these settings they had to be strong, independent, and responsible. These conditions created in them an inner strength and resiliency, as well as a deep wellspring of gratitude for what they did have. Traumas, such as family problems, losses, or serious illness, may have created inner wounds or demanded much from you, leaving you with the challenge of finding ways to cope and heal. Happy experiences can also create memories that can sustain you and give you hope when things go wrong. All of these possibilities can play important roles in how you feel toward yourself and how you view the world and your place in it.

The values you were taught. Your parents, grandparents, or clergy might have taught you to turn the other cheek, respect your elders, be polite, and put the needs of others before your own. In addition, most faith traditions encourage us to override our fears, anger, and grasping tendencies in favor of compassion. In Jewish literature, for example, Hillel states that the essential message of the Torah is to refrain from doing to others that which is hateful to yourself (Katz and Schwartz 1997, 33), a lesson that is repeated in the New Testament as the familiar instruction to do unto others as you would have them do unto you (Matt. 7:12). Buddhism expands this concept to be all-inclusive, instructing us to be motivated by love born out of concern for all sentient beings (Dalai Lama 2005).

Conflicting messages. At the same time, you may have observed your role models behaving with a "do as I say, not as I do" attitude. And then there can be conflicting messages between what we were taught at home, such as kindness and concern for others, and the influences of the outside world, where we may hear that it's a "dog-eat-dog" world where "nice guys finish last."

Interacting with people from different cultures can further complicate the matter, especially when it comes to interpersonal behavior. For instance, in many Eastern societies, behaving in ways that make you stand out (for instance, being assertive with an authority figure) can be interpreted as being arrogant or disrespectful, and can shame your family. An illustration of this is the Japanese saying that "the nail that sticks up the highest will be struck down by the hammer," which cautions people against drawing attention to themselves by, among other things, being assertive. In many Western cultures, by contrast, we are encouraged to use clear, direct, firm verbal language, and to stand up straight and make eye contact.

That Certain Indefinable Something

Sometimes the whole is greater than the sum of its parts. This is true for the arts and literature, and it is also true for who you are as a person. We all intuitively understand that in addition to the combined influences that science can count and measure, there is a mysterious something special that contributes to what makes you unique. Indeed, when it comes to your behavior, thoughts, feelings, interactions, and relationships, understanding the complex whole is certainly more than a matter of adding up its discrete components. As a therapist, I can attest to the fact that people are able to develop strengths and abilities that cannot be accounted for by the different variables that the science of psychology measures. And I am sure that you have known talented and remarkable people who come from very humble beginnings and yet are able to accomplish much more than their backgrounds might have predicted. Trust that you, too, can discover inner strength and power you never knew you possessed.

Contemplating the Beauty Within

The layers of experience and influences that guide how we think, feel, and behave can at times make it difficult for us to know how to handle situations, which can then affect how we relate to and feel about ourselves and others. The question of who we really are and what we are really made of reminds me of a true story about an ancient plaster Buddhist statue in Bangkok, Thailand, in the 1930s (Miller 2005). Although the statue was crude and not very attractive, a decision was made to move it from its original location in a shabby building with a tin roof to a beautiful new temple. During the move, a severe storm caused the workers to drop the statue into a large muddy area. The next morning the head monk returned to clean the statue and examine it for damage, and as he did so the plaster cracked open and revealed a beautiful gold statue beneath its rough exterior. Upon investigation, it was discovered that several hundred years earlier the golden statue had been protected from theft by invaders by covering it in plaster to disguise its true value.

Like the golden statue, your inner strength may have been covered by the mud and plaster of negative emotions and beliefs, hidden from view, even from yourself. The good news is that the rough surface of self-protection that has prevented you from having gratifying relationships with others can be chipped away. This can be accomplished by identifying and working with the grasping, hostile, or delusional inclinations that we all have so that you can increasingly rely on the inner goodness and wisdom that has always been with you. This is why the Buddha refers to all of us as "nobly born" individuals whose greatest assets are the pure open sky of our awareness and the goodness that is an intrinsic part of our own true nature.

An Invitation: Identify Negative Reactivity

Can you remember a time when you were driving a car and someone cut you off and nearly caused an accident? In that moment of fear and immediate physical danger most likely your reflexes took over. How did your body respond? Did you hit the brakes and/or have to swerve out of the way? Did you notice physical reactions, such as your heart pounding and palms sweating? What thoughts went through your mind? What emotions came into play? Did you decide that the other driver was a terrible person who had wronged you? Did you look for some feature, such as age, gender, or ethnicity, with which to condemn that person? Or were you able to hold back from judging him or making assumptions about his intentions, mobilize compassion, and think to yourself, "Maybe that person didn't see me" or "Perhaps he was preoccupied with a problem"?

Choosing Your Own Path

With all the various influences in our lives, it's no wonder that it might be hard for you to know when to speak up and what to say when you feel frustrated, angry, taken advantage of, or misunderstood. This dilemma, which so many of us confront, shows how nuanced and subtle human interactions can be and how hard it can be to mobilize our intellect and compassion when we are under stress. However, I believe that you can successfully navigate the tricky waters of interpersonal relationships if you trust that cultivating kindness and compassion will help you live a happier and more fulfilling life.

As you consciously cultivate these qualities within yourself, you will improve your ability to maintain a calm and caring presence with others—from loved ones to strangers—even when you are upset. Then, when a salesperson is rude to you, when your boss criticizes you, when you and your friend or partner have a disagreement, or when your kids get on your nerves, you can recognize and rein in aggressive or judgmental reactions. In addition, you can train yourself to consider that—just like you—others have their good days and their bad days, weaknesses and strengths, fears and hopes. Over time and with practice, when conflicts arise it will become easier and easier to respond to others in a reasonable, thoughtful, kind, and respectful manner, just as you would hope they would do for you.

○ *Ted and Dorothy's Story*

Ted and his wife, Dorothy, provide a good example of how we bring our own backgrounds and biases to our relationships and how by identifying and honoring our differences we can move past judging others so that we can benefit from each other's perspectives. Ted and Dorothy came to see me because of marital conflict. Their conflicts were especially intense regarding the differing child-rearing styles they used with their daughter, Sandy, who had learning disabilities, impulsivity, and several related behavior problems. Ted was raised in a large and authoritarian family with strict rules that included responsibility, respect, and obedience. He felt strongly that Sandy should be brought up to be a responsible and respectful person. In contrast, Dorothy was an only child whose parents were permissive, egalitarian, and very attentive to her feelings and preferences. She felt that her and Ted's most important job as parents was to be supportive and understanding toward their daughter and that if they set an example by being loving and generous, Sandy would develop those qualities too. Each parent felt that the other was damaging their child: Ted believed that Dorothy's leniency was preventing Sandy from becoming a responsible young woman, and Dorothy believed that Ted was harming Sandy with excessive and inappropriately severe criticisms. Whenever Sandy was belligerent toward Ted, he worried that Dorothy was undermining his authority and driving a wedge between him and his daughter. Meanwhile, Dorothy's main concern was protecting her daughter from what she felt was the destructive impact of Ted's authoritarian manner.

A turning point in our work occurred when instead of just criticizing each other, the parents began to appreciate each other's very different upbringing and personality, which led them to express their parental responsibilities in different ways. Once Ted and Dorothy could see that neither of them intended to harm Sandy or each other, their hearts began to soften toward the other. Gradually, they began to show appreciation toward each other for their good intentions, with concern for the other's frustrations. This allowed them to parent Sandy more as a team than as opposing forces. Sandy began to notice that her mother respected and honored Ted's firm expectations and that Ted appreciated the attention to Sandy's feelings that Dorothy's gentle approach demonstrated. Ted and Dorothy's effectiveness as parents gradually improved as they recognized that Sandy needed both the gentle love and firm parental leadership that they could jointly provide.

An Invitation: Give Others the Benefit of the Doubt

Can you remember a time when someone—coworker, relative, friend, or even a stranger—did something to you that upset you? Reflecting upon what was discussed earlier in this chapter, think about the possible causes and conditions that might have contributed to the person's behavior, including biological and genetic factors, as well as past life experiences and current challenges.

Can you bring a feeling of compassion to the burdens that might have contributed to the person's upsetting behavior? See if you can acknowledge your own feelings while consciously cultivating an attitude of unconditional friendliness toward him.

Consider the Implications for Your Interpersonal Style

- If you have an enthusiastic interpersonal style, remember as you read this book that you are not helping others by either consistently pressing your point or by avoiding addressing important matters. Trust that your compassion will help you bring up your concerns, or respond to the concerns of others, in a caring way.

- If you are in the discerning group, you may have difficulty giving yourself or others the benefit of the doubt. It will benefit you to focus on cultivating loving-kindness as a primary goal as you read through this book and to allow your wisdom to help you see situations clearly, especially the positive qualities that live in us all.

- If you are in the open-minded group, you may at times be oblivious to your own needs or the needs of others. As you put the lessons in this book into practice, try to be more tuned in to the difficulties that others may be having and focus on ways that you can work together to solve problems. Know that your open heart and mind can help you take everything in and help you resolve problems in a balanced and harmonious manner.

In this chapter you have seen that your interpersonal style is more complex than you may have thought—and less solid, independent, and permanent. Many variables can create new causes and conditions with the potential to help you to learn and grow. It will be important to acknowledge and respect your biology, genetic tendencies, and past experiences, but you do not need to be bound by them. Your freeze, fight, or flight reaction may jump to the foreground in times of stress, but the reasoning and caring parts of your brain can be trained to override aggressive or escape reactions. Understanding your interpersonal style (enthusiastic, discerning, and/or open-minded), including both your vulnerabilities and strengths, can help you find your own path to loving-kindness, wisdom, and equanimity. You have the power to be strong yet kind, even if you don't think that you do. With new knowledge and skills, you can chart a healthier course for yourself. And you can use compassionate assertiveness, introduced in the next chapter, as your compass.

CHAPTER 2

Compassionate Assertiveness: Improving Communication and Solving Problems with an Open Heart

How do we balance our competing needs to be compassionate and caring on the one hand and, on the other hand, to speak up, share our concerns, and assert ourselves when it is appropriate? It is not always easy to use kindness and compassion when things don't go our way, to be able to talk about our concerns, or to know when to promote our own agenda and when to let go. These are goals that most people strive for but often need help attaining. Compassionate assertiveness can help you develop the knowledge and skills you need to achieve these goals.

The Foundations of Compassionate Assertiveness

Compassionate assertiveness is a blend of the emphasis on concern for others found in Eastern philosophy, most notably Buddhism, and elements of

Western psychology, especially cognitive behavioral therapy. Let's begin by looking at a few key aspects of these two major contributors to the compassionate assertiveness approach and at how they gave compassionate assertiveness its name.

Buddhism

Siddhartha Gautama—who would later be known as the Buddha—was born near the border between Nepal and India over 2,500 years ago. He was a prince who gave up a life of luxury to pursue a spiritual path. After studying with a number of monks and religious teachers for several years, Gautama realized that others did not hold the answers to his questions, and he set out on his own to achieve higher consciousness and inner peace. He endured many trials, but by courageously cultivating awareness, compassion, and patience Gautama gained many brilliant insights and achieved the status of a Buddha, which means "enlightened" or "awakened" one. He spent the rest of his life working with groups of monks who could carry on his teachings and show others how to follow the same path.

The Buddha's teachings rest on the principle that we all engage in "afflictive" thoughts, attitudes, and behaviors that create suffering for us. He emphasized that by identifying and releasing ourselves from the roots of suffering (especially grasping, hatred, and delusion) and nurturing the roots of happiness (compassion, loving-kindness, wisdom, and equanimity, among others) we can bring peace, harmony, and, yes, happiness, to our lives and our relationships.

The "compassionate" part of compassionate assertiveness. Compassion, a very important aspect of Buddhist philosophy, is based on the principle of nonharm toward others. Compassion involves a deep sense of caring for the welfare of others, or, as they describe it in ancient Buddhist texts, a "quivering of the heart" in response to suffering or pain. It is a spontaneous reaction that comes from a feeling of deep connection with others and from our clear awareness that we have all at times experienced similar fears, frustrations, and sorrows. It includes personal love and caring for those we are close to, but ultimately its purpose is to have the deep wish for everyone to be free from suffering.

Cognitive Behavioral Therapy

Cognitive behavioral therapy (CBT) contributes the "assertiveness" ingredient of compassionate assertiveness. This branch of psychology works with the ongoing and reciprocal interactions between our behavior, feelings, thoughts, and physiological processes. The process includes recognizing problematic reactions to life's challenges and acquiring a variety of healthier and more effective responses in their place. CBT emphasizes corrective learning experiences and skill building. Let's look at some of the key elements in both the behavioral and cognitive aspects of cognitive behavioral therapy that contribute to the compassionate assertiveness approach.

Behavior. The "behavior" part of cognitive behavioral psychology emphasizes behavior and physiology and identifies two basic kinds of learning that are relevant to our interactions with others. The first is called classical conditioning. It addresses the emotional "false alarms" evoked by certain situations—extreme or irrational negative emotions, such as fear or anxiety, and their related physiological stress reactions, including rapid breathing, a pounding heart, and sweaty palms. These can lead to unnecessary avoidance or other harmful reactions that make us feel safe at that moment but ultimately increase our fear. Classical conditioning as part of CBT involves retraining the nervous system by gradually exposing a person to the feared situation so that his or her emotional and physiological systems become "desensitized" or "habituated" to it. This form of treatment can include relaxation, breathing exercises, or bringing attention to one's emotional discomfort without overreacting to it. For instance, if you tend to avoid bringing up problems for fear of rejection, this approach can desensitize you to your fear and help you override your tendency to avoid these situations.

The second form of learning relevant to our work in this book is called operant conditioning, an approach that emphasizes motivation. Operant conditioning includes ways that people's behavior can be influenced by whether or not it is reinforced, including our relationships and interactions with others. For instance, let's say a child asks his mother for candy at the grocery store in and has a temper tantrum if she says no. If the mother then gives in to him and buys the candy, it is likely that he will repeat this behavior because he will remember that he was rewarded for it in the past. A cognitive behavioral therapist might help the mother develop a behavioral plan to reward her child with praise or as part of an allowance system when he accepts "no" for an answer instead of giving in to the child in response to a temper tantrum.

Cognitions. The "cognitive" part of cognitive behavioral psychology helps us recognize our irrational or unrealistic beliefs or attitudes and see how those unhelpful thoughts affect our emotions and behavior. For example, suppose you are afraid to ask a neighbor if you can borrow a cup of sugar because you are worried that she will think you are irresponsible for not planning ahead. A cognitive approach would be for you to challenge that assumption, to consider other possible responses that your neighbor might have, and then to test your hypothesis in the form of a behavioral experiment by knocking on her door, making the request, and seeing what happens.

Assertiveness. Assertiveness training is basically a cognitive behavioral approach. It emphasizes the importance of understanding what might be holding you back and encourages you to stand up for yourself and to avoid giving in to the unreasonable expectations of others.

The assertiveness training approach was developed in the 1960s and '70s, when cultural and political changes challenged the status quo. It was an era of equal rights and political movements, the most prominent being the Vietnam War protests, the women's movement, and the civil rights movement. At home and in public, differing values regarding politics and respect for authority created clashes between parents and their teenage children, and between classmates, neighbors, and coworkers. Even individual self-expression—such as long hair on teenage boys—became a point of conflict in many families. Those were especially turbulent years, when conflicts boiled over. Ironically, these conflicts often occurred over issues involving equality, peace, and love!

During this same time, many mental health professionals stepped forward to apply the issue of equality to interpersonal interactions. *Your Perfect Right*, a book on assertiveness training, was first published in 1970 by Robert Alberti and Michael Emmons. It is now in its ninth edition and occupies space on the bookshelves of most cognitive behavioral therapists. Assertiveness training emphasizes asserting your rights (while also respecting the rights of others) and teaches how to exercise your power to make your own decisions and to exert more control over your own life.

The Four Basic Principles of Compassionate Assertiveness

On some levels Buddhism, with its philosophy of nonharm and compassion, and cognitive behavioral therapy, with its emphasis on the science of learning and skill development, are very different. But they actually have a lot in common. The areas where they overlap give us four underlying concepts that will be incorporated throughout this book:

1. *Actions are the result of complex causes and conditions.* Our responses to any situation in life are greatly influenced by our past and current circumstances. These complex causes and conditions contribute to our habitual mental and emotional responses to life's challenges, which in turn influence our future actions.

2. *Actions have consequences.* Whatever you do (or don't do) has consequences. These "actions" can be internal (feelings, thoughts, or sensations) or observable (your behavior, including how you speak to or about others). The consequences (positive, negative, or neutral) can be obvious or subtle, immediate or distant. And this process is repeated because each time you do (or do not) take a certain course of action, a new set of causes and conditions is created.

3. *Intentions matter.* Both cognitive behavioral therapy and Buddhism acknowledge that intentions matter whenever we say or do something that affects another person. Understanding and coming to terms with our own intentions, cultivating attitudes that entail more virtuous intentions, and making an effort to refrain from assuming that others have negative or selfish intentions are all important aspects of compassionate assertiveness.

4. *Follow the middle way.* Buddhism and CBT teach us that we should resist extremes, because doing so offers us the surest path to health and happiness. In fact, most psychological and interpersonal

difficulties are caused when certain thoughts, attitudes, emotions, or behavior are excessive or deficient. Too much or too little of even the most positive actions or qualities, then, can create problems for you and your relationships. This principle encourages you to think about whether you have *reasonable* expectations of yourself and others and to use flexibility and moderation in your interpersonal interactions.

Why It Is Not Selfish to Be Assertive

Perhaps you were raised to believe that speaking up for yourself, making requests of others, or expressing concerns is selfish. But if you have good intentions then at times it may important to be assertive in your interactions with others, as long as it is done in a calm, nonjudgmental, and caring way. Why is this the case?

Your Welfare Matters

You may be surprised to learn that according to Buddhist principles, your commitment to nonharm, compassion, and loving-kindness begins with you! The Buddha reportedly said that you can search the whole world ten times over and never find a person more worthy of compassion than the one right here: yourself. This is seconded by the Dalai Lama, who helps us understand that caring about and respecting ourselves is a kind of prerequisite for feeling that way toward others (2005). This is, at least in part, because just as we are imperfect, so are others. Therefore, by being patient and kind to our flawed selves we can train ourselves to be that way with others when they disappoint or hurt us.

Buddhism instructs us to be aware of and attend to our own needs, to protect ourselves from harm, and to treat ourselves with the same degree of loving-kindness that a mother would extend to her most beloved child. In fact, meditations on compassion and loving-kindness traditionally begin by sending loving wishes toward ourselves, as in the following example:

May I be free from hatred and suffering.

May I be free from inner and outer danger.

May I be healthy in body and in mind.

May I be filled with loving-kindness.

These words reflect a heartfelt intention to care for your own welfare and well-being. According to Buddhist philosophy, it is only when this message resonates within you that you can fully extend it to others.

Compassionate assertiveness applies this principle to our interactions with others, recognizing that nonassertive people who do things against their will, hold back from taking care of themselves, or allow themselves or others to be mistreated cannot really be happy, peaceful individuals. In fact, rather than always being placid saints, they may at times use unhealthy means to get their way or show their disapproval through passive resistance or by developing a sour or avoidant demeanor. Nonassertiveness can have serious emotional consequences as well, including anxiety, depression, and low self-esteem.

○ *Tony's Story*

Tony was raised to be extremely thoughtful and respectful, especially toward his elders. The youngest of several children, he took the Sunday school teaching "turn the other cheek" to mean that only through self-denial and complete obedience to authority figures could he be a worthwhile human being. As an adult, Tony came to see me because he had become increasingly aware of and uncomfortable with how his boss took him for granted and how some of his friends took advantage of his generosity. He was not sure about what was fair or right and wanted guidance. As we worked together, over time, he realized that he had never fully developed a sense of himself as someone worthy of respect and love and that this interfered with his ability to assess whether others' expectations of him were reasonable. With his increased awareness that he had a responsibility to himself to be treated with thoughtfulness and consideration, over time Tony began to set limits and to say no when others asked more of him than he felt was reasonable.

The Welfare of Others Is at Stake

In addition to being responsible for our own welfare, Buddhism teaches us that we must also look out for the welfare of others. You might think this means allowing others to get their way all the time. But believe it or not, being assertive with others can actually increase their welfare and happiness.

The principle that you have some responsibility for the welfare of others as well as yourself is included in the Eastern religious belief called *karma*. According to that belief, what happens to you in the present is a consequence of what you have done in the past. And what you do in the present creates new conditions (karmic "seeds") that will affect your future. (This concept of personal responsibility is also found in the West in such maxims as "as you sow, so shall you reap" or "what goes around comes around.") So if you stand by idly while a child, spouse, or coworker behaves in destructive or unkind ways toward others, you are at least partly responsible for the negative "karmic debt" that is created.

Therefore, when you are assertive with someone in a caring way, you can actually be performing an act of compassion. Even though at times it may take courage for you to assert yourself, it is easier to do so when your intention is to prevent a person's misguided behavior so that he doesn't have to suffer negative consequences, either in the short run or in the long run. In addition, his behavior may indicate that he is a troubled individual or ignorant of certain social rules. This means that your constructive effort can help him if it is done in a way that will guide and support him.

Another important point is to intervene with compassion and understanding, whether or not you like the person. From a Buddhist perspective, you should respond to everyone, not just your favorite people, in the same caring way that you would hope to be treated, even if you had done something hurtful to them (Dalai Lama 2005).

The Buddhist karmic concept that actions have consequences corresponds to the "ABC's" of cognitive behavior therapy. "A" stands for antecedents, the circumstances that precede and trigger certain behaviors. "B" stands for the behavior (including thoughts and things you say) that is a response to the antecedent. And "C" stands for the consequences or outcome of the behavior. This is a simple way to remember that what we do, why we do it, when we do it, and how we do it matter and have consequences. Given the overlap between this aspect of cognitive behavioral therapy and Buddhism, is it any wonder that the Buddha can be thought of as the first cognitive behaviorist?

An Invitation: Investigate Causes and Conditions, Intentions, and Consequences

Think about a time when someone harmed you, intentionally or unintentionally. Did you do anything about it? Contemplate whether there were any consequences for either of you and whether the person ever apologized to you or tried to make amends. Looking back on it now, what is your understanding of the causes and conditions that might have contributed to her behavior?

Now (this may be harder to do) think about a time when you intentionally or unintentionally harmed another person. What causes and conditions do you think led to your behavior? Were there any consequences? Looking back on it now, how do you feel about what happened?

Finally, think about a time when you observed someone harming another person. Consider some of the possible causes, conditions, and intentions that might have led that behavior. Did you do anything about it? If so, what did you do, and if not, what held you back? Were there any consequences for you or either of the other people? Looking back on it now, what are your feelings about what happened?

○ *Beth's Story*

Beth's story illustrates the importance of taking responsibility and taking a stand when it is important to do so. As you read about her, notice how her assertiveness was not selfish, and be aware of the four compassionate assertiveness principles: (1) actions are the result of complex causes and conditions, (2) actions have consequences, (3) intentions matter, and (4) follow the middle way.

A lovely and kind woman with a husband, James, and a teenage son, Paul, Beth had a long history of difficulty asserting herself with both her child and her husband, as well as with others. One of the concerns that she brought to me was her husband's tendency to drive aggressively, which she felt put him and others on the road in harm's way. When she addressed this concern with him, he justified his behavior by blaming other drivers for cutting him off, tailgating, or driving too slowly.

Over time, Beth's concerns increased, as did her expressions of concern. She recognized that James had a lot of built-up anger due to problems he had faced as a child, so she encouraged him to seek counseling, but he did not. Using our work with compassionate assertiveness, Beth gradually came to see that she had a responsibility to ensure her own safety and that of others, as well as to help James avoid the consequences of causing a potentially serious accident. She slowly realized that what she had said and done up until that point was not strong enough to keep everyone safe.

After one especially harrowing incident, Beth was finally able to take a strong stand with James. She now knew that if she did not act in a protective manner, should anything terrible ever happen, she would be partly to blame. She told him that she admired many of his driving skills, but that when he became angry with someone on the road, he became an unsafe driver. Although she could not force him to go to counseling or stop him from driving aggressively, she felt the situation was so unsafe that she could no longer ride with him, nor would she allow Paul to, until James had successfully received counseling for road rage. Despite James's protests and the increased driving that this meant for her, Beth held firm. In this way she demonstrated both compassion and assertiveness: she took responsibility for her own safety and the safety of her son, husband, and others on the road, but did so in a thoughtful and compassionate manner.

Consider the Implications for Your Interpersonal Style

- If you have an enthusiastic interpersonal style, your gracious nature may cause you to deny problems or avoid conflict. It will help you to remember that if your intentions are to help everyone involved, the other person will benefit from your skillful and caring handling of differences or concerns.

- If your interpersonal style is that of the discerning group, being aware of your concerns may not be difficult for you. What may be a challenge for you is bringing them up in a way that conveys that you care about the other person's welfare.

- If you have an open-minded interpersonal style, your uncertainty about what to do and what not to do may cause you confusion, and a desire to put problems out of your mind. Therefore, you will need to discipline yourself to address your concerns when appropriate, and make hard decisions.

As discussed, it is not always easy to maintain compassion and to assert ourselves in a thoughtful and calm manner when we are angry, afraid, or confused, but it can be done. Using the detailed guidance in the following chapters, you can develop the tools you need to master the art of expressing yourself and looking after your own welfare, and the welfare of others, with confidence and compassion. Although the work may seem daunting, the good news is that if you are willing to put time and effort into shifting your perspective and learning new skills, the lessons that follow can help you build healthier relationships and a happier life. Now that you have a basic understanding of compassionate assertiveness and the benefits it can offer you, in the next section of this book we will explore the inner work that you will need to do as you prepare your mind and heart for the journey.

PART 2

Training Your Mind
and Your Heart

CHAPTER 3

Gratitude: Foster Appreciation to Reduce Negativity

You can think of learning about and applying compassionate assertiveness as embarking upon a challenging personal journey, one that begins by cultivating inner strength and resiliency. The four qualities explored in part 2 of this book—gratitude, equanimity, courage, and forgiveness—can play an important role in this process by giving you the tools you will need to develop a strong and caring presence when dealing with others, not only when things are going well, but also when inevitable problems arise. Let's begin with gratitude.

How Grateful Are You?

Gratitude is one of the most important contributors to happiness (Emmons 2003), and is also a necessary ingredient in the practice of compassionate assertiveness. Do you consider yourself a grateful person? Let's find out just how grateful you are. Take the following gratitude survey, developed by Michael McCullough, Robert Emmons, and Jo-Ann Tsang (2002), major researchers in the field of positive psychology.

An Invitation: Assess Your Level of Gratitude

To understand the role gratitude plays in your own life, take a moment to complete the survey below. Choose how much you agree with each statement. Using the scale below as a guide, write a number beside each statement to indicate how much you agree with it:

1 = Strongly disagree

2 = Disagree

3 = Slightly disagree

4 = Neutral

5 = Slightly agree

6 = Agree

7 = Strongly agree

_____ 1. *I have so much in life to be thankful for.*

_____ 2. *If I had to list everything that I felt grateful for, it would be a very long list.*

_____ 3. *When I look at the world, I don't see much to be grateful for.*

_____ 4. *I am grateful to a wide variety of people.*

_____ 5. *As I get older, I find myself more able to appreciate the people, events, and situations that have been part of my life history.*

_____ 6. *Long amounts of time can go by before I feel grateful to something or someone.*

Instructions for scoring:

Add up your scores for items 1, 2, 4, and 5.

Reverse your scores for items 3 and 6 because they are stated in a negative rather than a positive way. (That is, if you scored a "7," give yourself a "1," if you scored a "6," give yourself a "2," etc.)

Add the reversed score for items 3 and 6 to the total for items 1, 2, 4, and 5.

Your total score should be between 6 and 42.

Your score reflects your level of gratitude. About 50 percent of those who have taken this quiz received a score of 39 or above. Are you satisfied with your score? Unless you got the highest possible score of 42, you can always improve upon it. And as your score goes up, most likely your level of happiness and the quality of your relationships will too. Let's see why.

The Impact of Gratitude on Your Relationships

Gratitude not only enhances your inner sense of well-being, it also improves your relationships and your interactions with others (Emmons 2003). If you have an "attitude of gratitude" it will make people want to be around you. Your number of friends will increase. And your appreciation of them will very likely increase their appreciation of you, too.

Individuals who are grateful for the good things in their lives seem to draw people to them; their positive attitude is contagious and magnetic. G. K. Chesterton, an English writer who lived in the late 1800s and early 1900s, is a good example of someone who personified gratitude. He came up with such statements as "I would maintain that thanks are the highest form of thought; and that gratitude is happiness doubled by wonder" (2001, 463) and "The test of all happiness is gratitude" (1986, 258). Despite being clumsy and a poor student as a boy, and very absentminded and forgetful as an adult, he appreciated life and lived it to the fullest. It is no wonder that he was surrounded by friends and well-wishers.

Chesterton provides a good role model for us. However, as with many good role models, it isn't always easy to live up to his standards. Although you might wish to be in touch with the gratitude you feel toward the people in your life, this can at times be hard to do, especially when you feel angry, frustrated, or hurt. But luckily, gratitude is a skill that can be developed with practice, so if you are willing to put in some effort you really can retrain your brain to appreciate the people who at times may annoy you but who at other times gladden your heart and give you joy.

Gratitude's Role in Compassionate Assertiveness

What does gratitude have to do with compassionate assertiveness? First, by focusing on your gratitude before discussing a concern or problem with a person you will be more likely to:

- Be in touch with the ways in which the other person has enriched your life, which will soften your anger

- Recognize that the other person's flaws are only a small part of who he or she is

- Give the other person the benefit of the doubt, and hold back from assuming negative intentions

- Be able to bring up the issue in a friendly and caring manner

Secondly, when you express appreciation for the other person's positive qualities and contributions to your life, then on occasions when you thoughtfully bring up concerns the other person is more likely to:

- Want to retain your high regard by being responsive to your needs

- Listen to your concerns without becoming aggressive

- Respond positively to your requests

- Make an effort to seek a mutually agreeable solution

    o Be influenced by your modeling caring communication and use the same thoughtful approach with you when you do something upsetting

Developing a high level of gratitude is important in your relationships, not only because it will enhance your life, but also because it will protect you from the flip side of that coin: if you have a low level of gratitude you are more likely to take the positive qualities of other people for granted and may spend a lot of your time and energy complaining to them about their flaws in ways that could compromise your relationships.

How to Increase Your Level of Gratitude

If gratitude is an important ingredient in happiness and healthy relationships, how do you increase its presence in your life? Both positive psychology, a relatively new form of cognitive behavioral therapy (Seligman 2002), and Buddhist philosophy take the position that increasing your gratitude—and reaping its rewards—is a skill that you can learn and one that with ongoing practice can continue to grow throughout your life. Here are some steps to increasing your level of gratitude:

Step 1. Wake Up to Gratitude

Buddhist writers sometimes use the metaphor of sleep to describe how out of touch with reality we can be. We often drift through our days on automatic pilot, only partially tuning in to what is going on within us and around us. This concept is so key that one of the translations of *nirvana*, or enlightenment, is "awakening." In the context of gratitude and relationships, this includes awakening to all that you have been blessed with, including the people in your life.

How awakening to gratitude helps you cultivate compassionate assertiveness. Remembering what you are grateful for in a relationship can help you think about problems without being swept away by fear or anger, because you are better able to look at the whole picture.

Step 2. Contemplate Gratitude

Once you wake up to gratitude, you will be able to consciously focus on the good things in life and in your relationships on a day-to-day basis. You can begin to do this by exposing yourself to intellectual and cultural experiences (such as literature or movies) that celebrate the gifts of family, love, and friendship. Bet even more important, take some time to think about people who have contributed to your welfare—not only in new relationships but those who nurtured you during your growing-up years as well. Remind yourself that in spite of their limitations, there were parents, relatives, neighbors, and teachers who supported and cared for you during your youth and that there is almost certainly at least one way in which each of them wants you to be happy and well. This reservoir of goodwill is something you can dip into as you think about your complaints and dissatisfactions in your relationships. If you remember the positive qualities of the people in your life, it will be much easier to express your concerns when problems arise because they will be given and received in a larger context of respect and appreciation. One way to nurture gratitude is by using a guided meditation such as the one that follows:

An Invitation: Meditate on Gratitude

Sit comfortably in a quiet place where you are unlikely to be interrupted. Once you are settled, take a few full breaths to help you feel grounded and centered and slowly read the following passage silently or aloud. Include the actual names of individuals and modify the text in any way you want in order to better capture your own personal experiences.

> *I offer my gratitude to the people who have enriched my life and helped me become who I am today. I am thankful that their human limitations—and mine—have not kept them out of my heart.*
>
> *I gratefully acknowledge all who have gone before me: my ancestors and elders; my grandparents, relatives, and parents. I give thanks to the many sacrifices they made so that I could receive whatever food, shelter, and other comforts they were able to provide for me. I offer my gratitude for the lessons they have taught me, and for the wisdom they have shared. I am grateful for whatever measure of love and caring I have received.*

I offer my gratitude to my siblings/husband/wife/partner/friends, who have shared their lives with me. I am thankful for their caring presence in my life. I am grateful for the happy times we have shared and also for the difficult times that we have faced together. I offer my gratitude for the many qualities that they embody—for their acts of loyalty, kindness, humor, and generosity.

I give thanks to my children/students, whose lives have given me so much purpose and meaning. I offer my gratitude for the joy they have given me and for the lessons they have taught me. I am thankful that they have helped me increase my patience, generosity, and kindness. I am grateful that I am able to guide them and to help them grow up to be strong, loving, and capable adults.

I offer my gratitude to my teachers/neighbors/coworkers/supervisors/subordinates. I am thankful for their support and encouragement and for their contributions to our shared accomplishments. I appreciate the criticisms and guidance that have helped me improve myself. I am grateful for the opportunity to work, so that I can meet my responsibilities with dignity.

I am thankful for the strangers/customers I encounter every day in the community. I offer my gratitude for those who have offered a friendly smile and a helpful hand. I appreciate the difficult people who gave me an opportunity to cultivate forgiveness, kindness, and patience. I give thanks to those in need for giving me the opportunity to be of help.

I offer my gratitude.
I offer my gratitude.

Gratitude meditation is a practice that has been used by Buddhist monks for centuries. Despite poverty, hardship, and at times even persecution, in assessments of gratitude and happiness these monks have extremely high scores (Flanagan 2006). Their simple lives provide us with dramatic evidence that a lot of the things you may assume you need in order to be happy may not be as important as you think. On the other hand, the connection you have with others, which you may take for granted, is one of the greatest gifts of all.

How contemplating gratitude helps you cultivate compassionate assertiveness. Reading or listening to such passages as the one above can begin to influence the way you think about others and about the many connections you have with people you encounter every day. If those connections include gratitude, it will decrease stress levels in your interactions with them. This, in turn, will help you feel more comfortable in giving and receiving understanding when others (or you) are not at their best.

Step 3. Write It Down

Another way to cultivate gratitude is to keep a gratitude journal. In one study, college students were randomly divided into two groups. One group was asked to write gratitude entries in a journal on a regular basis, while the other group was instructed to write about hassles. The results were significant: compared to the "hassles" group, the "grateful" group reported more energy, determination, joy, and enthusiasm. They also had fewer health complaints, spent more time studying, were more optimistic about their future, and felt better about their lives as a whole. Furthermore, they were more likely to offer support to others (Emmons and McCullough 2003).

Following the lead of these researchers, I now regularly encourage my clients to write in what I call a "positive journal" for just a few minutes a day, with a goal of five entries daily. I ask them to not only write down things they are grateful for but also note the acts of kindness that they do for others, as well as document heartwarming or positive things that they observe others doing.

Because it is hard for many people to bring the positives onto their radar screens, I often begin my sessions by having clients read from their positive journal or at least talk about what has gone well since the previous session. Once they get used to this routine, they usually notice that doing the exercise improves their mood and their attitude toward others. And writing these things down rather than just mentally noting them allows people to review the positives from prior days and weeks, especially when they are feeling sad or discouraged, and to recognize their progress. One woman told me with some pride that out of curiosity she went back and reread early entries from several months prior and was surprised to see how much her awareness of the positives in her life had increased over time.

An Invitation: Keep a Positive Journal

Try writing in a positive journal for at least two weeks, preferably on a daily basis, for about five minutes per day. Keep it with you during the day and write in it when time and circumstances allow, or put it next to your bed and write in it before you go to sleep. In addition to writing down general items, include at least a few entries of appreciation for a person in your life. The statements can be broad or very specific. At the end of the two weeks, consider continuing your positive journal, making it an ongoing part of your daily routine. The five minutes a day you spend writing in your positive journal is a small investment of time that will reap large benefits.

When you are upset with others, see if it is helpful to look at entries regarding those people so that any criticism, request, or limit setting can be done in the context of caring. You can also go back and read entries from the past when you are feeling down or to review your progress.

○ *Maria's Story*

Maria came to me for help with chronic anxiety, low self-esteem, and depression. Although she had had many ups and downs in her life, she also knew that she had much to be grateful for—she was an attractive, accomplished professional with many friends, was close to her family, had a strong spiritual life, and was financially secure. Despite these positives, though, she had great difficulty focusing on the good things in her life. I asked her to begin keeping a positive journal. She did, although reluctantly, and would read from it during our sessions. Slowly, her mood began to improve.

One week she arrived at our appointment close to tears, with her first statement being "It's been a miserable week!" I responded that I wanted to hear about the challenges but first wanted her to read to me from her journal. "I forgot to bring it. Anyway, there haven't been any," she lamented. I waited. Finally she said, "I went to church and after the service I thanked the people who supplied the delicious food that we had afterwards." Pause. "Oh, and I called the dentist about a billing error. I told the office person that I appreciated the fact that in all the years I had been going there, this was the very first time there had ever been a problem." She started to smile. Her voice trailed off. I asked her to focus on that day, which would still be fresh in her mind. Silence ensued for a minute or so. I gently urged her on, "Think small—the tiniest positive. It can even be something you just observed." After a minute, her eyes lit up. "Well, it was a beautiful day…and someone at work who has been a bit of a thorn in my side helped me out with a last-minute request that I made, so I am thinking about her in a different way now." "That's great work," I replied. "Your gratitude, balanced approach, and acts of kindness are already there, just waiting for you to remember and acknowledge."

The rest of the session was very productive, and Maria was able to mobilize optimism that what she could do over the next few weeks could help her continue to build up and act on an increased level of gratitude. We also discussed some challenging issues, including some difficulties she was having with her neighbors. Later in the session she agreed to continue writing in her positive journal so that she could refer to it when she felt down and to try to remember to bring it to our next session so we could review it. By the time she left I could see that her mood was significantly better than it had been at the beginning of our meeting. I believe it was the focus on the positives that shifted the tone and gave her the energy to work on the issues she had brought to the session.

How writing it down helps you cultivate compassionate assertiveness. Our brains are designed to notice and remember the negatives much more than the positives, so when you write down the positives in your life, you are better able to retrieve them later. At one time or another we all have been criticized by another person who did not take our positive qualities into account. Think about that, and maybe it will inspire you to write down appreciative comments about others. Then, when you are upset with someone, go back and read some of your own entries to help you balance your perspective.

Step 4. Express Gratitude When Someone Is Kind to You

Recognizing that you are grateful is just half of the job. It reminds me of an old saying that feeling grateful but not expressing it is like wrapping up a gift and not giving it. I try very hard to be generous with expressions of appreciation and gratitude and have never regretted doing so, even toward people I don't especially like. I have advised the people who seek my counsel to do the same, including expressing appreciation or gratitude to people with whom they do not get along. This can require some work, because, as mentioned earlier, when we are upset with people we tend to forget about their positive qualities. However, if you are seeking to be a happier and more content human being, there is no downside to letting people know that you recognize, appreciate, and are touched by their positive qualities and acts of kindness. In other words, when it comes to expressing gratitude, if you think it, say it.

How expressing gratitude helps you and others. As mentioned previously in this chapter, if you express appreciation for the other person's positive qualities on a regular basis, then when you bring up concerns in a friendly and caring way, the other person is more likely to respond in a positive manner.

But there are additional pluses as well. Expressing gratitude to others is a declaration that you know you are fortunate to have people in your life who are kind to you and can inspire you to strive to be more like them. In addition, it is gratifying for others to hear your words of appreciation, which in turn will bring you joy. Finally, your expressions of thanks will encourage them to continue these acts of goodness, not only for you but for others as well. To use a Buddhist metaphor, you are sowing positive karmic seeds, which will grow and blossom and will, at some point, directly or indirectly, result in positive consequences for you. In other words, as the Dalai Lama says, you are being "wise selfish," which is a very good thing (2005).

In his book *Authentic Happiness* (2002, 74–75), Martin Seligman describes a lovely technique for expressing gratitude. Several of my clients have done this exercise with very good results. Perhaps you would like to try it, too. It may have a very powerful impact on both you and the person to whom you are grateful:

An Invitation: Communicate Your Gratitude

Write a one-page letter of gratitude to someone who has made a significant positive impact on your life. If possible insert it into a plastic sleeve, frame it, or laminate it. Arrange to visit that person, without saying anything about the letter. After visiting for a little while, slowly and expressively read the letter out loud, frequently looking up to make eye contact with your listener. Then give him or her the letter, and allow plenty of time for the listener to respond. Stay for a while, and talk together about what you have written and about that person's meaning in your life.

Step 5. Transforming Gratitude into Generosity

Gratitude naturally flows into generosity. A Jewish sage once asked the following riddle: "Who is a wealthy man?" Answer: "One who is happy with what he has" (Shapiro 2006). This is applicable to relationships as well as to material goods. And when you are feeling truly appreciative, it may feel as if your cup "runneth over," (Psalms 23:5) and your acts of generosity will flow naturally.

When your partner, a member of your family, a friend, or someone at work is kind to you, in addition to thanking him or her, see if you can look for ways to return the kindness or "pay it forward" by helping others. Helping those you are close to is an obvious outlet for these feelings, but as you become more and more grateful for what you have, you may find that your interest in reaching out beyond your inner circle will grow. A warm smile, an offer of help to someone who is carrying heavy packages, and an expression of concern and support to someone who is sad or afraid are all opportunities that will become more and more apparent. On a larger scale, you may decide to do volunteer work for a cause or organization that you believe in, knowing that the time, energy, or money spent is not really lost, but invested in something important. The position you are taking is that giving is not losing, but a form of sharing that enhances rather than diminishes your life. And if you are really feeling generous, try making an anonymous gift or donation. In the Jewish tradition this is considered one of the highest forms of charity, because you give without expecting praise from others and avoid potentially embarrassing the recipient (Dossick 1995).

Generosity will bring you joy and will create the awareness that what you do in this world matters. As Jack Kornfield puts it so well in his book *The Wise Heart* (2008, 201), you are not generous in order to be good; you are generous in order to be happy. And keeping in mind that actions have consequences, trust that your acts of generosity will reap benefits for your relationships that go far beyond the immediate joy that they bring you.

How generosity helps you cultivate compassionate assertiveness. By being generous, you are also laying the foundation for healthy assertiveness, because you are communicating a positive, caring, and respectful attitude toward others. Then, when the inevitable time comes that you need to assert yourself or set limits with people in your life, you can do so with the awareness that we all deserve to be corrected in a benevolent way, when we make a mistake.

Consider the Implications for Your Interpersonal Style

- If you are in the enthusiastic group, your gratitude for the people in your life may at times overflow. However, you may cling to the expectation that things should always go well, and when you are feeling left out, taken for granted, or otherwise upset with others, your challenge will be to remember that getting your way may not always, or ultimately, be in your best interest.

- If you are someone in the discerning interpersonal group, your most important challenge will be to soften your focus on the negatives or ways to improve others, open your mind and heart to the qualities of others, and remember that—just like you—they sometimes stumble.

- If you are a member of the open-minded group, your challenge will be to pay more attention to the many benefits the people around you bring to your life and to remember to express appreciation and reciprocate.

To quote Johannes A. Gaertner, author and theologian, "To speak gratitude is courteous and pleasant, to enact gratitude is generous and noble, but to live gratitude is to touch Heaven" (1994, 18). Consciously increasing and expressing your gratitude and appreciation for the positive qualities in others in words and deeds is in itself one form of generosity. This might require you to dig deep, especially with those individuals who create difficulties for you. However, the more you do it the easier it will become. Over time and with lots of practice you will be able to "live gratitude," and it will be much easier for you to be assertive in a compassionate way when problems arise.

In this chapter you have received the first of several tools: the knowledge that gratitude, as well as generosity, will help you cultivate compassionate assertiveness. In the next chapter we will explore the topics of equanimity and patience, two more tools for your compassionate assertiveness "toolbox."

Chapter 4

Equanimity: Stand Firm, Compromise, or Let Go

In the previous chapter we explored the compassionate assertiveness tools of gratitude and generosity and how they can help you have more fulfilling relationships. In this chapter we will discuss equanimity and patience and how they can help you maintain a balanced perspective in the face of frustrations you may have when interacting with others.

The Two Arrows of Suffering

Buddhism refers to the inevitable ups and downs in life by using the analogy of being struck by two kinds of arrows. The "first arrows" are the inevitable problems in life that give us physical and emotional distress, which is generally translated as "suffering" (also referred to as "pain" or "unsatisfactoriness"). Events ranging from getting caught in traffic due to a car accident, to not being invited to a party, to learning about the serious illness of a loved one are examples of first-arrow pain. Our basic emotional reactions to these events, such as anger, frustration, fear, and sorrow, also constitute first-arrow pain.

The second arrows of suffering include overreactions, misguided attitudes or assumptions, misinterpretations, and judgmental reactions related to events that caused first-arrow suffering. Although they may seem justified or even necessary at the time, sooner or later they usually make problems worse and increase our pain. Outrage at people who had the nerve to get in an accident and make you late for an appointment, the assumption that not being invited to a party means the hosts don't like you, and self-loathing for not having treated someone better in the past are all examples of second-arrow suffering.

The remainder of the chapter will explore frustration, a first-arrow form of suffering, and how some of its corresponding second-arrow reactions—impatience, intolerance, and pride—can harm our relationships. We will see how equanimity and patience, two more tools of compassionate assertiveness, can help you overcome these problems.

When First-Arrow Frustration Leads to Second-Arrow Suffering

Frustration occurs when your efforts to achieve a desire or goal are foiled. We all experience frustration from time to time—for instance, when the computer doesn't cooperate—or when we have trouble finishing a puzzle or a project. In these cases, although frustration may run high at the moment, it is usually put aside once the situation changes, the problem is solved, or the project is abandoned.

Frustration as it applies to our interpersonal interactions is more complicated. Imagine that someone—knowingly or unknowingly—does something that annoys or irritates you. Frustration, then, is the first arrow. When frustration occurs in relation to interpersonal matters, we can often feel the sting of its second arrows: *impatience, intolerance,* or wounded *ego*. These reflect a judgmental focus on the other person instead of a healthy and honest observation of our own thoughts, feelings, and actions.

Buddhist philosophy tells us that much of the second-arrow suffering we experience is related to our emotional emphasis on "me, myself, and I" and our false perception that our experiences and welfare are independent from those of other people. Thoughts and attitudes that fuel that perception include the belief that the needs of others are less important than yours, that your identity is tied up with being right, and that there is only one right way (yours) to solve a problem. These ways of thinking (and we all fall into them from time to time) can create barriers between you and others.

Frustration can also be related to a zero-sum game mentality, an attitude that one person's gain requires an equal loss for the other person.

When your mind is in that competitive place it's all too easy to start thinking in dualities: mine/hers, win/lose, right/wrong—all of which contribute to second-arrow suffering.

Although these tendencies can be seen in aggressive individuals, they also occur in nonassertive people who become frustrated because they feel (sometimes accurately) that they almost never get their way. They may experience impatience, intolerance, and pride, but instead of asserting themselves, they seethe with resentment and may engage in avoidance, passive resistance, or withdrawal.

An Invitation: Investigate Impatience and Intolerance in Yourself and Others

Bring to mind a situation when you felt impatient or intolerant toward someone. What were the causes and conditions that led you to feel, think, or behave that way? What were your intentions? What were the consequences, if any? Looking back on it now, how do you feel about it?

Now bring to mind a time when someone was impatient with or intolerant of you. How did you feel at the time? Can you think of any causes or conditions that led that person to behave that way toward you? What do you think his or her intentions were? Were there any consequences for you or the other person? Looking back now, how do you feel about what happened?

We all have the capacity to understand the second-arrow thoughts and emotions of impatience, intolerance, and pride and to be vigilant when they threaten to undermine our ability to express ourselves in caring and effective ways. And one of the most important tools that we have toward that end is *equanimity*.

Equanimity to the Rescue

Equanimity, which was discussed in chapter 1, involves the ability to step back emotionally from a given situation and examine all aspects of it in a balanced, dispassionate, clear, and calm manner. It emphasizes your ability to be aware of the big picture without being distracted or swept away by fleeting perceptions, thoughts, or emotions. It also involves not being overly attached to external positives (such as praise, success, pleasure, or fame) or overly reactive to their negative counterparts (insults, failure, pain, or disrepute). Johannes A. Gaertner captures this concept in his statement that "Equanimity is won by seeing all things in their proper perspective, including our own life" (1994, 27).

Equanimity is an antidote to frustration, and equanimity is also the path to patience, because if you look at any given situation with an open mind, you will find that there is much more to consider than your own personal perspective. And when this is done, patience is a natural outcome. There are many wonderful metaphors for the spacious and stable qualities of equanimity, including those that use imagery from nature. One such metaphor is that of the sky, which is unchanging above the clouds and storms that pass through. Another is the metaphor of a mountain, stable and rooted to the earth, able to retain its identity and basic form despite changes in the seasons. A third metaphor is that of the still surface of a clear lake, which reflects everything—clouds, birds, stars, and moon—without being affected by the objects reflected on its surface (Kabat-Zinn 2005; Kornfield 2007).

The dispassionate nature of equanimity is not the same as behavioral passivity or cold detachment. Nor does equanimity mean that you should be resigned to endure endless frustrations in life. Rather, you can use it to help you recognize and work with frustration as well as the second arrows of impatience, intolerance, and pride. Equanimity and patience acknowledge that frustration may be inevitable at times but that it is possible to experience it as an opportunity to cultivate inner strength. This is especially applicable to our relationships, because under the watchful eye of equanimity you can begin to make thoughtful, wise decisions about what to do when you are frustrated: whether, when, and how to let it go or be assertive.

Managing Impatience

Impatience is a common expression of frustration and often involves judging other people. You can become impatient when your child's dawdling makes you late for work or a waitress makes a mistake with your order. But one of the best examples of impatience, and one that most of us can relate to, is being delayed while driving because of construction, an accident, or a slow driver ahead of you. Our reaction to this kind of situation reminds me of a quip I once heard that patience is something that you admire in the driver behind you but not in the one ahead of you.

An interesting point about impatience is that it often mobilizes our self-centered ego, such as when we believe we could do whatever it is better than the other person or wish that we could control him or her. When we are impatient we often lack empathy for the causes and conditions that might be contributing to someone's flaws, forget that the other person has no intention of harming us, or develop amnesia regarding the times we have done exactly the same thing. Impatience can lead you to take action in ways that alienate others or that you may otherwise regret. At times it can even lead to aggression.

The opposite of impatience is, of course, patience, which is identified as a virtue in almost every culture and religion. In the wisdom traditions there is recognition that cultivating patience is much more likely to lead to a win-win situation and to the peaceful resolution of problems by compromising or letting go than is an impulsive expression of impatience. As this Chinese proverb instructs, "If you are patient in a moment of anger, you will escape a hundred days of sorrow."

○ *Amy's Story*

Amy had a million errands to run. Some of them were last minute, and some were really important. But first, she couldn't resist making a side trip to a clothing store that was having a big sale. She grabbed the last blue blouse in her size, quickly tried it on, and was delighted with how good it looked on her. Then, just before she got to the cashier, she made one brief stop to look at a pretty belt. She decided against it, but during the minute that she paused, two people got to the cashier ahead of her, and each of them had an armload of clothes. In addition, someone who was standing nearby stepped in front of Amy just as she approached the line. Worse yet, the cashier had some problems with the cash register and each item had to be rung up by hand.

What Amy had thought was going to be a quick trip to the store during a busy day became an exasperating experience. If she looked inward she might have been able to identify such second-arrow judgmental and impatient thoughts as "Hey, that woman butted in front of me. What nerve!" or "That idiot cashier, what incompetence!" as they bubbled up in her mind. When this happened, the focus of her energy was basically on what was wrong with the other people. This, in turn, fueled a false duality of "me versus them," "right versus wrong," or "good versus bad." But had she been aware of the processes of her mind, she could have actually transformed the experience into an exercise in patience.

When feeling impatient, we can use equanimity to help us remain steady in the face of frustration. In Amy's case, her frustration and impatience might have reminded her that maybe next time she should allow more time to run errands or that she could let go of one of her errands and relax. Or it might have led her to remember times when she, too, had quickened her pace to get in line before someone else, or times at work when people were impatient with her, and to recall how that felt to her. And as for the woman who stepped into line just as Amy got there, she could have used the principle of the middle way—avoiding both the aggressive extreme of yelling out "Hey, I was here first!" and the nonassertive impulse to automatically step back (if it was clear that the other woman had jumped the line).

In similar situations, I have trained myself to consider that I might have been in error, smile at the other person, and ask, "Oh, were you here before I was?" Nearly every time I have done this the other person has replied, "Oh, sorry, please go ahead." But on the few occasions when they did say, "Yes, I was," I was prepared to yield and said, "Oh, sorry. Go ahead." After all, I might have been mistaken. And if not, there may be causes and conditions that made the person behave that way. In Amy's case, equanimity could help her ask herself, "In the grand scheme of things, does this five minutes really matter?" to regain her perspective. Or using a bit of equanimity and patience might have led her to decide that she could live without making this impulsive purchase and walk away.

Managing Intolerance

Equanimity can also help you manage intolerance, which usually involves a feeling of superiority over other people. If you ever ask yourself whether you are being intolerant, notice whether you are putting other people down, rolling your eyes, or gossiping about them. If so, then the answer to your question is probably yes.

Intolerance often comes up when we encounter people we do not identify with—people who may be in a different ethnic or socioeconomic group, have different religious beliefs or political affiliations, or look or act differently from the way we do. Intolerance usually includes judging others, especially if we believe that their situation or attitudes are due to a moral failing we ourselves would never exhibit. But intolerance doesn't come up only with strangers or people we don't like; even those we love can evoke those feelings, including our children or disabled or elderly relatives who embarrass or frustrate us.

In its extreme, intolerance can also include contempt or disgust. I had to confront this prejudice in myself years ago when I encountered certain people who were less fortunate than me. When I was younger I dismissed their needs, justifying my unkind attitude by telling myself they were inferior to me in some way. Now I feel very differently. I think about all the causes and conditions that can lead people to desperate straits and ask myself whether I would do much better if I had the exact same genes and life experiences.

Using Equanimity to Manage Intolerance

Equanimity can help you ask yourself why you are feeling intolerant. Perhaps you feel uncomfortable with that person who is overweight, disabled, elderly, or poor because on some level it frightens you to think that, but for fortune, this could have happened—or someday might happen—to you. Other times you may be so focused on your own problems that it feels too challenging to absorb the problems of others, and you find yourself blaming them for their limitations so that you won't feel guilty. Let's see how this can happen.

o *William's Story*

William was a busy husband and father of two young children. His elderly widowed father was in poor health, and because his eyesight and reflexes had deteriorated he no longer drove and rarely left his house except to take short walks in the neighborhood. He had his groceries delivered to him, and he hated going to the shopping mall, even when someone drove him there.

One fall weekend William's dad took his winter coat out of the closet and realized that it had several moth holes in it. He panicked because this was his only overcoat and the weather was too cool to wear a sweater. He called William and asked him to go to the store that weekend to buy some coats for him to try on at home. Unfortunately, that particular weekend was especially busy for William because of his daughter's soccer game and a dinner party that William and his wife were having. In addition, William's sister, who usually helped out, was out of town, so she couldn't pick up the slack.

Ordinarily, William would have been happy to run this errand. But under these circumstances he found himself having several intolerant thoughts about his father, such as "Why wasn't he more careful with his coat?" or "He's being too demanding and not thinking of my needs."

Few of us are proud of ourselves when we reflect honestly upon our intolerant thoughts and feelings. But although it may sound counterintuitive, if you allow yourself to be in touch with them in a compassionate way it will help you shift to a more patient attitude. And by having the courage to think about where feelings of intolerance are coming from, you can open the doors of understanding.

In William's case, mobilizing equanimity and awareness of his intolerance and resentment led him to understand the causes and conditions that were in play. He then considered that he may have been warding off sadness about his father's decline, guilt that he was too busy to help him, or a deep-down painful awareness that some day he, too, would be sick, old, and dependent on others. He also reminded himself that his father very rarely asked anything of him except for a visit a few times a month.

While it is difficult to look at parts of yourself that are not pretty, equanimity can soften your self-judgment while also mobilizing the question of what it would be like for you to be in another person's shoes. And it is most helpful to both you and others when you can hold your own negative and uncomfortable thoughts, beliefs, and feelings in the tolerant and gentle heart of compassion.

Equanimity and patience can help you be assertive in a respectful and caring way. This doesn't have to mean dropping everything in order to please someone, but neither does it involve reacting in a defensive or aggressive way. For William, maybe it would mean explaining to his father that he understood his sense of urgency but that it just wasn't workable for him to help out that weekend. He could tell his father that next week he or his sister could take him shopping or bring some coats to his house and help him try them on. Coming from a place of equanimity and compassion, William could be assertive but also caring and supportive. One would hope that William's father would feel okay about this plan, but even if he was angry with William for not being able to immediately meet his needs, William wouldn't have to take it personally. Instead, he could recognize that if he were in his father's position, he might be a little bit panicked and demanding too.

Managing Pride and Ego

Some kinds of pride can be thought of as healthy pride, such as the feeling of accomplishment from a difficult job well done or when your team wins a hard-fought game.

But there are other kinds of pride that can be problematic for yourself and others. One is the personal pride that is associated with ego, that self-absorbed state of mind we associate with arrogance, narcissism, vanity, and the belief that other people's needs are not as important as ours, or by actions motivated by the desire to be admired. And wounded pride can arise when you jump to the conclusion that someone is doing something on purpose out of disrespect or rudeness or just to humiliate or embarrass you.

Personal pride can be especially problematic when you feel competitive toward people at work or in your personal life. For example, do you find yourself wanting to prove other people wrong in order to gain admiration from those around you? Do you tend to want to have things your way because you think your opinion is better than everyone else's?

But despite its outward appearance of superiority, a prideful attitude can also mask insecurity. Second-arrow emotions such as jealousy or resentment over the accomplishments and good fortune of others can lead us to search for things to criticize about them. This is a common problem, especially in our competitive society. I remember one workshop I went to where the presenter was talking about a topic that was one of my areas of expertise. She was a very articulate and attractive woman, and her presentation was outstanding, yet I felt irritated with her. I found myself looking for flaws in her, but the best I could come up with were such thoughts as "Well, she really doesn't have very good taste in clothes." Then, aware of what I was doing, I thought, "Whoa, where did that come from?" A quick check-in with myself revealed that I was feeling threatened and jealous, and that I had been looking for something—anything—about her to criticize. Once I became aware of my own threatened feelings and wounded ego, I completely softened and opened to my own vulnerability, which then allowed me to enjoy and appreciate both her and the rest of her presentation.

I now try to check in with myself whenever I feel critical of someone. This has helped me explore my darker emotions while simultaneously showing compassion for myself, which then, somewhat paradoxically, allows my negative feelings to dissolve. Furthermore, now when I work with clients who struggle with this issue, I can listen and respond with compassion, recognizing that they, along with me and millions more, are in the same boat.

The desire for status among our peers is hardwired, so we can expect pride and ego to reveal themselves from time to time. Ironically, though, those who are humble and self-effacing are often the ones who gain the most respect from others. The Dalai Lama is revered as someone who treats everyone he encounters, from heads of state to impoverished children, with equal respect, warmth, caring, modesty, and interest. And this lack of ego allows him to act without pride and arrogance. In one lecture that he gave in front of thousands of people, someone asked the Dalai Lama a complex and subtle question. He paused for a moment, and then with much laughter responded, "I don't know!" The audience loved it (Dalai Lama, 1997).

This self-effacing quality is not limited to famous people. Some time ago I heard about a man who had a reputation for being the ideal dinner partner. People raved about how much they enjoyed talking with him and always looked forward to his company. When asked what made him so appealing, they invariably brought up how much interest he showed in them and their ideas and how engaged he was in learning more about them, making them feel like they were the only one in the room. Instead of trying to prove to everyone how fascinating he was, he spent his energy communicating to everyone else how fascinating *they* were. This was very enlightening to me because it showed how he connected with people in a nonthreatening and interested way. By not elevating himself, he ended up being elevated by others!

o *Lucy's Story*

Lucy's son Jim was never great at picking up after himself, and now that he was a teenager it seemed that everything had gotten worse. He spent hours combing his hair but left his wet towel on the bathroom floor and the sink area in a mess. He changed his clothes twice a day but left them lying around. Lucy and her husband had to nag Jim to do just about everything and were dismayed by his tendency to "blow them off."

One day a friend stopped by for coffee, and when she left Lucy went into the bathroom. As she turned on the light she saw that Jim had left his wet towel and underwear on the floor and the uncapped toothpaste on the sink despite Lucy's explicit reminder to clean the bathroom after himself. Even worse, her friend had used the bathroom! Lucy's irritation and embarrassment led to thoughts that included assumptions of intention: "He is purposely defying me" and "He doesn't care about my needs or feelings." She also began to expand her criticism of him, counting his many flaws with increasing emotional heat, and began planning a significant punishment for when he got home.

Let's see what happens when the four principles of compassionate assertiveness help you when others have caused you humiliation or hurt your pride. In Lucy's case, can she let herself acknowledge the causes and conditions that may have contributed to her son's behavior that particular day? Can she step back from assuming that his intentions were to create problems for her? Is she able to use the concept of moderation to find a reasonable consequence for his negligence in order to help him learn a valuable lesson, rather than one motivated by her own personal annoyance and embarrassment?

Perhaps you have had similar experiences with your children, or even with a roommate or partner. Actions have consequences, and for Jim's sake and for Lucy's, something had to be done. The first goal, though, was for Lucy to avoid being driven by anger or negative assumptions about Jim's intentions. The second goal was to design a consequence intended to be a good learning experience for him rather than a vehicle for revenge.

One way to avoid overreacting in such situations is to think back to your own teen years and the developmentally expectable self-absorption that you probably experienced. See if you can remember how thoughtful, considerate, and respectful you were regarding the needs of the other people in your family. If you were responsible and thoughtful toward others, what causes and conditions helped you be that way? Cultivating an empathic and open frame of mind, rather than an ego-based one, will help you discipline your child without adding fuel to the negative feelings that you may be harboring.

How Equanimity and Patience Can Help You Let Go

When we feel the first-arrow suffering of frustration, or the second-arrow suffering of impatience, intolerance, or wounded pride, equanimity and patience can teach us to step back and look at the whole picture and to remember that as human beings, we all have fears, desires, hopes, and flaws. Just as we are at times unfairly judged by others, so, too, do we at times unfairly judge others, especially when they do or say something that interferes with our lives or makes us uncomfortable. Keeping little phrases in mind can help us be more patient and tolerant when we are feeling annoyed or insulted by someone. Some of my favorites come from Charles Mansueto, the director of my clinic, who—when appropriate—makes such comments as "No one is everybody's cup of tea" or "We all have our little quirks."

This does not mean that you should necessarily ignore frustration or related emotions, because if we are aware of our feelings they can be pointers to internal or external problems that need to be addressed. Compassionate assertiveness recognizes that infinite accommodation of others is not always possible or even a good thing, for you or for others. There are times when in the best interests of all it is important to leave a situation, speak up, negotiate, set limits, or take action. The trick is to do it in a skillful and patient manner and be conscious of our intentions. This includes shining a light on our very human tendency toward negative emotions and assumptions about others, and then trying to understand the causes and conditions that underlie these feelings. Thinking about frustration, impatience, intolerance, and pride this way will give you a broader perspective, and will help you respond with the best that is within you.

An Invitation: Cultivate Equanimity

Think again about the invitation earlier in this chapter, in which you were asked to contemplate a situation where you felt impatient or intolerant. Now bring equanimity to the front of your awareness. If at that time you had been able to look at the whole picture with clarity and an open heart, would you have felt or behaved differently?

Consider the Implications for Your Interpersonal Style

- If you have an enthusiastic interpersonal style, it may be relatively easy for you to use equanimity and patience in many situations, but pride may be your stumbling block, so be especially aware of opportunities to cultivate humility and noncompetitiveness when you are in a situation where assertiveness may be needed.

- If you have a discerning interpersonal style, you have the awareness, wisdom, and integrity to recognize the importance of equanimity, especially when it comes to being aware of your own prejudices. Your greatest difficulty may be impatience with people who are less competent than you are, so be ready to work with that tendency in situations that call for assertiveness.

- If you have an open-minded interpersonal style, your challenge may be to increase your awareness of subtle impatience, intolerance, or pride within you that may creep in under your radar. However, since equanimity is one of your strengths, once you are aware of frustration, impatience, intolerance, and wounded pride you will have a relatively easy time working with these afflictive emotions.

In this chapter we have explored how we can all fall prey to impatience, intolerance, and ego-driven pride. Using patience and equanimity is easier in some situations than others. When you feel frustrated, you might be able to add the qualities of equanimity and patience to those of gratitude and generosity, which were described in earlier chapters. But can you mobilize these virtues in really tough circumstances? What about when you feel angry or frightened and don't know if you have the courage to speak up? In the next chapter we will explore how to face and work with these difficult emotions.

CHAPTER 5

Courage: Face Your Fear of Conflict

An important Buddhist incantation includes the words "May I be free of suffering and the causes of suffering." As discussed, according to ancient Buddhist teachings, suffering is a kind of malady that is fueled when certain emotions—such as anger or fear—get out of hand. And when this happens, these overwhelming feelings can create major problems for us, interfering with our ability to address problems we are having with others. Compassionate assertiveness involves finding the courage to respond to anger and fear in constructive ways; but to explore this we will need to look in more detail at the causes and conditions that fuel these negative emotions.

The Beauty and Baggage of Our Biology

In chapter 1, you read a bit about how your nervous system reacts to perceived danger. We will now take a closer (albeit simplified) look at how your brain reacts to the stress of facing potential conflict. In particular, we will focus on how your neuroendocrine system (the combination of your nervous and endocrine systems) responds to a variety of events, affecting your feelings, thoughts, and behavior. To begin we will look at the three interconnected parts of your brain that are most involved in your relationships and interactions with others: the reptilian brain, the limbic system, and the cerebral cortex, which will be described using an evolutionary perspective (MacLean 1990).

The Reptilian Brain
(It's All about Survival)

The most primitive part of the brain is sometimes called the "reptilian brain" because it controls the automatic, reflexive survival and reproductive behaviors that are most clearly seen in reptiles. It includes the brain stem—an extension of the spinal cord—and (from this evolutionary perspective) also the hypothalamus. When there is a sense of danger, your reptilian brain signals your body to *freeze* while your sensory system takes in relevant information. Meanwhile, it ramps up the sympathetic (*emergency responder*) nervous system so that if needed, you can fight or flee. Here's how it works: Let's say someone cuts you off when you are driving and nearly causes an accident. Your reptilian brain almost immediately receives the signal that the situation is potentially dangerous. Then it signals the release of stress hormones and other chemicals, including noradrenaline and adrenaline (also called norepinephrine and epinephrine) and cortisol. You begin breathing more rapidly and your heart rate speeds up as blood is channeled to your limbs, lungs, and heart in order to deliver these chemicals and extra oxygen to those areas. This increases your ability to react with strength and speed and—if needed—with aggression. This "fight or flight" response, which takes place in less than a blink of an eye, is a function of what is called the *sympathetic nervous system*. In the case of the potential auto accident, hopefully you avert the accident by slamming on the brakes or swerving the car. If all goes well, once the crisis is over the *parasympathetic* ("rest and digest") part of your nervous system helps your body gradually calm down and resume normal activities.

The Limbic System
(Feelings Matter Too)

The limbic system (sometimes referred to as the "old mammalian" part of the brain) nestles above the reptilian brain. Many nerve tracts go to, from, and through the limbic system, connecting and communicating with different parts of the brain, including the reptilian brain and the cerebral cortex. In addition, the limbic system itself serves a number of functions found mostly in mammals, including bonding, protecting and nurturing one's offspring, and processing emotions, such as love, anger, pity, and fear. The amygdala, one of its key structures, can be thought of as a dispatch center that gets the rest of the brain and body ready for fight, flight, or freeze reactions. In this way the limbic system provides an emotional context (fear, anxiety, panic, anger, or rage) when threats are perceived..

In an emergency situation, such as the near accident, in addition to the instinctive reptilian brain reaction of our sympathetic nervous system, your amygdala also leaps into action. A variety of emotions may flood in, including fear, anger, or even outrage. When we are caught up in the grip of our neuroendocrine system's responses, the addition of strong negative emotions, such as rage, can lead to impulsive acts of aggression. In fact, some people might even chase after the offender in order to get revenge by honking angrily, tailgating, or worse. And if you have ever been on the receiving end of such anger, you might know what it is like to experience fear on a very basic level.

The Cerebral Cortex (Your Thinking Brain)

The cerebrum is a part of the brain that enfolds the limbic system. It has a wrinkly gray outer layer called the *cerebral cortex*—also called the neocortex, or "new brain," because it is most prominent in primates, especially humans. The cerebral cortex (most notably the prefrontal portion, located behind your forehead) is the crowning glory of human evolution because it organizes and modulates input and output between various parts of the brain and body. It is, therefore, involved in complex social interactions and relationships, emotional regulation, rational and abstract thinking, planning, imagining, spirituality, empathy, and problem solving—in other words, the processes we associate most closely with what it means to be human. This is also the part of your brain that makes it possible for you to communicate through the use of language and other symbols. It is the reason that you can comprehend the words on the pages of this book, and it gives you the ability to apply their lessons to your life. When we talk about the "mind," what we are generally referring to are the thinking processes that go on in this part of the brain.

How the Parts of the Brain Work Together

The different parts of your brain work together to give you the ability to manage a full range of situations effectively. Reptilian survival instincts run deep, however, and can influence your behavior more than you might realize. When you are stressed, anger and fear—the legacy of certain functions of your amygdala—can overpower the bonding and rational parts of your brain. Buddhism and other wisdom traditions, as well as modern psychology, can give you the frame of mind and the skill-based tools to work with and master these negative emotions when they get out of hand or do not serve you well. However, given how powerful our survival reactions are, the willingness to work problems out in a caring and peaceful way often takes courage, inner strength, and trust.

○ *Ben's Story*

Ben prided himself on his hard work at his job and on his many contributions to his company. One day he heard about an upcoming professional conference where he had given presentations in the past. He was thinking about asking his coworker Peter to join him in applying to give a presentation on a new technique that they had developed together; however, before he had a chance to ask Peter, someone told him that their boss had already talked to Peter about giving the presentation.

Ben was angry and deeply hurt. He could not believe that the boss had bypassed him and that Peter had not talked to him about what was going on. He felt betrayed and unappreciated, and he was tempted to leave for the day so that he would not run into Peter or his boss while his feelings were running so strong. Ben then began to ruminate about other times when he was upset by decisions his boss had made, and even worse, he began to have fears about his standing as an employee. He felt his chest tighten, his heart race, and his hands turn cold and clammy. He wanted to do something, but he was too confused and upset to even know where to begin.

Ben's response to feeling threatened is not a surprising one, since his stress reaction was part of his biological makeup. Now let's use a Buddhist perspective to see how this kind of stress response can affect all of us.

Two Common Arrows of Suffering: Anger and Fear

As described in the previous chapter, Buddhism uses an arrow analogy to describe pain and suffering, with "first-arrow" pain and suffering coming from the inevitable problems we all face in life, and "second-arrow" pain and suffering from the mental and emotional reactions piled onto first-arrow pain, which we do have some control over. In that chapter the focus was on the first arrow of frustration and its related second arrows of suffering: impatience, intolerance, and wounded pride. In this chapter we will concentrate on the first arrows of anger and fear, biologically driven emotions fueled by the sympathetic nervous system. In this chapter we will concentrate on the first arrows of anger and fear, biologically driven emotions fueled by the sympathetic nervous system when a threat to our well-being is perceived. We will also explore the related feelings and thoughts of second-arrow suffering and discover how you can begin to free yourself from them.

The Heat of Anger

The first arrow of anger is an automatic response to threats to ourselves or those with whom we have a bond. When limited to the objective facts of an immediate situation, anger is not a bad thing; it can let you know that something is wrong and needs to be attended to. In fact, although the Dalai Lama warns us against hatred, even he recognizes that anger's energy can motivate us to recognize and do something constructive about a problem (Dalai Lama 2005). However, how you deal with and express your anger makes all the difference between whether you are able to constructively solve a problem or make it worse.

Anger is generally a reaction to a past event, and it reflects your emotional and cognitive interpretation of the event's meaning. For instance, imagine that you believe someone said or did something unkind to you, and your initial reaction is anger. If you use that anger as a signal that a problem may exist, it can energize you to find a solution. However, if your reptilian brain and your amygdala take over and react to the problem as if it were a threat to your survival, then your mind is likely to get caught up in second-arrow suffering. You might wrongly assume hurtful intentions or malice, which can then lead you to do things that may not be wise or in your best interest. This could include adrenaline-driven actions such as storming in and screaming at her, or making a hasty and ill-conceived plan to never speak to her again or even seek revenge.

Unfortunately, locking the other person out of your heart is seldom the answer. You can think of this kind of anger as a kind of "hot" negative energy that can take on a life of its own and create even more pain and suffering for you. The Buddha used the metaphor of grabbing a hot coal when he described holding on to anger, making the point that while we might intend to throw it at someone else, we are the ones who get burned.

The Cold Grip of Fear

Just as the first arrow of anger can signal a problem you need to respond to, the first arrow of fear generally anticipates a future threat that needs to be avoided or prevented. In actual life-threatening situations, such as when there is an intruder in your home, fear may direct you to physically escape from real and immediate danger. But in normal day-to-day life, this is not the case. You may become fearful if you want to ask someone out on a first date, if you think your boss is angry with you, or if you suspect that a friend has betrayed you in some way. When something like this happens, you can expect that your reptilian brain, sympathetic nervous system, and amygdala will respond with fear, anxiety, or dread, but that doesn't mean you should always trust those signals to be accurate assessments of true danger.

While anger tends to be a "hot" emotion, fear is often experienced as cold. We all know that feeling: you are upset with someone but can't think what to say or do. The feeling gets worse, even though you try to shake it from your mind. You want to talk with the person but the words won't come. Instead of moving on, you may be frozen in anticipation of all the bad things that might happen. Your skin becomes clammy and you are filled with dread. Because you feel cut off from the other person, it is hard to approach him or her in a friendly way. Your fear may include the worry that whatever actions you take will backfire and lead to an escalation of the problem or even the possibility of estrangement.

Situations that elicit fear can also lead you to rehearse what you will do in the future. If the thinking and feeling parts of your brain can work together effectively you can make a plan, execute it, lay the problem to rest, and move on. But if you are like many people, even after you have a plan, you may get stuck in an endless cycle of reviewing or revising it, creating more and more potential scenarios and more and more worry. Your body may reflect this tension: as your sympathetic nervous system mobilizes, your muscles tighten, your blood pressure rises, your heart pounds, and your stomach ties itself in knots. Your thoughts, emotions, and sensations can feed on each other and send you into an unproductive spiral of anxiety and second-arrow suffering.

Anger and Fear Together: The Double Blow

Anger and fear can also be triggered simultaneously when someone does something that hurts you. Incidents that cause this kind of pain can be relatively minor, such as your loved one forgetting to tell you he'll be late for dinner after you made a special effort to cook his favorite meal. In this case you may feel angry that you wasted a special dinner but fearful that if you confront him that he will respond with anger or detachment. Or the incident can be more serious, such as a fight with siblings over a major financial matter. In this case, you may feel anger because you believe you are not getting what you are entitled to, but also feel fearful that if you press your demands it could destroy these relationships.

When anger and fear are both present, second arrows of suffering, including a sense of helplessness, depression, or even self-loathing, can also emerge. In these kinds of situations, your emotional experience of anger and fear can become overwhelming, leading to a kind of paralysis or "stuckness" that can weigh you down and drain you of energy—emotionally, mentally, and even physically. It can then be very difficult to summon the energy to make and carry out a constructive plan or even talk to the person about the problem.

When you feel angry, afraid, or a combination of both, can you count on your cerebral cortex to help you out? Maybe. Your cerebral cortex can be your ally or your enemy, depending on whether you have the ability to challenge the false beliefs your mind may harbor.

Your Mind: Servant or Master?

As discussed, your cerebral cortex, the thinking part of your brain, is part of what makes human beings unique and is one of your most valuable inner resources. And when it comes to your relationships with others, the language functions of your cerebral cortex can be awe inspiring. Your mind allows you to engage in complex verbal and written communication, participate in close and meaningful relationships, hold a job, and engage in life-affirming interactions with friends, family, people at work, neighbors, and even strangers. Your brain's language center also allows you to store and access memories, and to assess your positive qualities as well as areas that need work.

But despite the advantages of your intellectual gifts, you may be surprised to learn that you can't always believe what you think. This situation can occur when your mind:

○ **Misperceives or misunderstands what is happening.** Trusting your mind's appraisal of danger would be fine if it were always accurate. The problem is that it often overestimates the actual level of threat. Our language-based misperceptions, intuitions, and misunderstandings can cause us to misread many situations, especially when we are under stress (Gladwell 2005; Cline 2006). The unreliability of eyewitness testimony is a well-known example of this, and we all know that when we are in a highly emotional state we can tend to make false assumptions based on incomplete or inaccurate information.

○ **Overreacts or makes illogical assumptions.** Let's say you are angry over something that just happened and your mind jumps to the future and what you might do about it. Leaders in the field of cognitive therapy have coined many terms to describe mental errors that can keep you from accurately assessing and interpreting the situation. These include mind-reading (you think you know what other people's thoughts, feelings, and intentions are), black-and-white thinking (things are all good or all bad), fortune-telling (you think you can predict how others will respond to you), and emotional reasoning (if you feel a certain way, then it is reality) (Beck 1976; Burns 1999). When you fall into these traps, you are very likely to overreact and fall into blaming, judging, or even condemning yourself or others.

○ **Won't let go.** Imagine a time when you had a disagreement with someone. The incident is over, and the outcome was a good one or a not-so-good one. Unfortunately, even when the incident is past, the mind sometimes behaves like a hamster on a hamster wheel—around and around it goes, reviewing, regretting, ruminating, and "chewing on" the argument over and over again. Sometimes these mental reviews can continue to pop up months or even years later, trapping you in a prison of chronic stress. Worst of all, this can close your heart to the relationship and can even keep you from moving forward with your life.

○ **Blocks things out.** When we are overwhelmed, ambivalent, or confused by complex or emotionally charged problems, it can be hard to sort things through and come up with a course of action. In these situations, a kind of paralysis can set in. This may be a natural response (remember the initial neurological "freeze" reaction to threat?) if it buys you time to come up with a plan. However, some people find it very hard to release themselves from that state and may retreat into a passive sense of helplessness. If you get stuck for too long, you can remain in negative interpersonal patterns, or even destructive relationships, because you do not realize that you have the power to change things (Seligman 2002).

The Mind-Body Connection

At times the survival reactions of the reptilian part of your brain, the emotional fuel of your amygdala, and the cognitive distortions of your cerebral cortex can conspire against your best interests. This can make it so hard to keep a cool head and a warm heart in times of conflict that it can feel as if you are "swimming upstream" (Batchelor 2009).

For instance, imagine how you would feel if you heard that a friend had betrayed you in some way. The first arrow might be the pain of shock or anger when you heard about it. The second arrow could include the related thoughts that might roll around in your mind—such as worry that gossip is being spread about you, your friends won't respect you, or your friendship is now destroyed. Emotional reactions such as hatred, the desire to inflict humiliation, or planning revenge, also reflect second-arrow suffering.

These kinds of reactions can not only lead to more suffering for you but also have a broader effect. Just as acts of compassion and loving-kindness have a ripple effect, so too does hatred. When you reject or act aggressively toward someone, even if you think you are justified in doing so, it might lead the person to take revenge and escalate the negativity between you. Or it can cause the other person to take out his anger on others and thus continue the cycle of aggression. The Buddha expressed this succinctly when he counseled his followers to realize that "hatred never ceases by hatred, but by love alone" (Kornfield 2008, 214).

This doesn't mean that negative emotions or thoughts are necessarily bad; they have an important role in recognizing and solving problems. But if they are misguided or too intense, or continue for too long, they can prevent you from accurately assessing situations and addressing them in a balanced manner.

In stressful interpersonal situations, instead of ignoring, holding on to, or running away from your angry or fearful reactions, it can be valuable to consider that they may be signposts that need to be investigated. This is similar to what happens if your smoke detector goes off, even when you just light a candle. In that case you can investigate and determine that you don't need to run out of the house, because the smoke detector is giving you false information. While you can get a new smoke detector, you can't get a new brain; but you can retrain it so that you can recognize when real danger is present and when it is not.

The Price You Pay When Anger and Fear Get Out of Hand

When you feel angry or afraid, and your mind is telling you that someone is bad or out to get you, you might feel that these negative thoughts and feelings protect you or are at least justified. As mentioned earlier, strong and even painful emotions can give you important information that can lead you to take corrective measures.

But remember that when your sympathetic nervous system, negative emotions, and cognitive distortions mislead you, you are more likely to be hypervigilant—looking for problems that may not even exist—which will increase the likelihood that you will ascribe negative motives to others and jump to conclusions. During these times, you may be so focused on protecting yourself that you can easily forget your connection with the person you are angry with, who—just like you—is a mixed bag of strengths and flaws. When fear or anger dominates your thoughts, it can keep you from moving on or resolving problems, robbing you of the pleasure of being engaged in and enjoying life, not to mention getting a good night's rest.

Not only that, dwelling on fear or anger can lead to the overmobilization of the stress response and over time can actually undermine your health. A condition called "chronic stress response" has been implicated in medical problems including nervous tics, headaches, irritable bowel syndrome, high blood pressure, and a compromised immune system, as well as psychological conditions such as anxiety and depressive disorders (Mayo Clinic 2010).

When we look carefully we can see that the body speaks to us in many ways. When you are under stress, it is just as important to pay attention to your physical sensations as it is to attend to your feelings and your thoughts, because sensations, too, are pointers to your experience at that moment. If you can acknowledge their presence without becoming overwhelmed by them, they can teach you much about suffering and about how you can reduce suffering in your life.

How Compassionate Assertiveness Can Help

Is it possible to rein in and work with anger and fear and their related fight, flight, or freeze reaction? Is there any way to challenge your distorted thoughts and to mobilize the wisdom of your cerebral cortex and the positive emotional part of your limbic system when it is under stress? The answer to both of these questions is yes. You can begin by trying to examine your emotions, bodily sensations, and thoughts in a calm manner. This will allow your cerebral cortex and the bonding, nurturing part of the limbic system to play their valuable roles in accessing the lessons that compassionate assertiveness has to offer.

Using the Four Basic Principles of Compassionate Assertiveness

In chapter 2 you read about four principles that can guide you as you develop compassionate assertiveness skills. Let's apply these now to the problems of anger and fear, as illustrated by Ben's story earlier in this chapter, and see how compassionate assertiveness helped him with a potential conflict he had at his job.

Actions (and reactions) are a result of complex causes and conditions. Ben's anger and fears were caused by assumptions he was making regarding his boss and coworker. When he was able to take a step back and think more clearly, he realized several things. First, the information about Peter came from someone other than Peter or his boss. Ben did not know the details or even know if this information was accurate. He also acknowledged that he had not seen Peter or his boss recently and so did not know whether he was to be included and, if not, why.

Actions have consequences. Since he did not have full information, Ben realized that it did not make sense for him to make all kinds of assumptions. It was in his best interest, and in the best interest of his relationships with Peter and his boss, to find out what was happening and not to jump to conclusions that could lead him to behave in ways that he might regret. He made a decision to contact Peter and ask him about the conference and to keep an open mind.

Intentions matter. Ben made an effort to refrain from assuming that Peter and his boss were intending to leave him out of the plans. Even though his mind was casting about for negative explanations, Ben could not identify any instances in the past when he had felt pushed aside. Rather than assuming that he was losing status at work, he tried not to feel threatened. He would give Peter and his boss the benefit of the doubt and would approach Peter in the same friendly way that he would want to be approached if someone wanted to bring a concern to him. He also decided that his own intention was to stay calm and remain open to whatever transpired. If a problem was revealed, he told himself, he would give himself time to step back and think about it before saying or doing anything.

Follow the middle way. Ben knew that at times he had a tendency to avoid addressing concerns. He also knew that his avoidance often ended up leaving him feeling victimized or taken for granted, which in turn caused him to hold on to silent resentments. And sometimes when he held things back, his pent-up anger would lead him to avoid people or lose motivation to fulfill his responsibilities, which he knew was not in his best interest. He decided to neither ignore his concerns nor build up resentment that could work against his relationships.

Ben did approach Peter and asked him whether he was thinking about going to the conference. Peter said that the boss had just said something to him, not as a certainty, but as a possibility. Peter had asked the boss whether he and Ben could deliver the presentation together, but the boss said that he wanted to talk with Ben about it first, because there might be some other possibilities. Therefore, Peter had held back from saying something to Ben. They parted on a friendly note, agreeing to keep each other posted.

While Ben was mulling over whether or not to call his boss, the phone rang and it was his boss, asking Ben to stop by his office. Trying to stay calm, Ben sat down with his boss, who told him that although he wanted both Peter and Ben's ideas to be presented at the conference the company was on a tight budget, and Ben had gone in prior years, while Peter had not, so he was thinking that Peter should have a turn. Besides, the boss said with a smile, another conference was coming up in six months that Ben could attend and where he could deliver a similar talk. The boss felt that having each man go to one conference would be a cost-effective way to represent the company and spread the word about its accomplishments. The first conference was coming up fairly soon, and he had happened to see Peter and so ran the possibility by him. However, he had been waiting to find out whether they would have a time slot for the speech before solidifying the plan. He had just been given approval that morning, at which point he put the call in to Ben.

This outcome was a good one in terms of external events. But it was even a better one for Ben in terms of his feelings. He was very pleased that he had been able to rein in his fear and anger, which allowed him to stay calm while he worked to find out what was going on. Had his imagination run wild, he would have spent a lot of emotional energy on a problem that did not even materialize. Had there been a problem, he began to trust that he could have given himself time to figure things out in a calm manner.

An Invitation: Facing Your Fear of Conflict

Think about a time when you were upset about something but afraid to bring it up. How did your body respond? What beliefs or thoughts did you have about yourself or the other person? Do you think that the next time you have a problem with someone, you can ask yourself the following in order to manage your anger and fear?

- *Actions are the result of complex causes and conditions. Do I know that a problem really does exist? If so, could any part of the problem be my responsibility, and if so what are the causes and consequences that led up to it? What if I am jumping to conclusions and there is no problem?*

- *Actions have consequences. Is the other person aware of the problem? Are there any potential consequences of actions taken by either of us that I should keep in mind? What are the potential consequences if I overreact?*

- *Intentions matter. What are my assumptions about the other person's intentions? Might I be wrong about them? Are there other possibilities? Moving forward, what are my intentions? Can I tolerate the possibility that even with my good intentions, I still might not get what I want?*

- *Follow the middle path. Am I able to find a middle way to address my concern—to neither withdraw in fear nor build up resentment or a head of steam, but rather remember my common bond with the other person and approach the problem in a way that is friendly, respectful, and confident?*

> ### Consider the Implications for Your Interpersonal Style
>
> What are the unique challenges and strengths that you bring to problems that need to be addressed?
>
> - If you are in the enthusiastic group, your strength is in your deep concern for others. Your challenge is to identify when your fear about upsetting others keeps you from addressing problems with them in a direct manner, and to remind yourself that keeping quiet won't help them or you.
>
> - If you are in the discerning group, when you have a concern, you have the insight to make good suggestions, but first you may have to soften that critical and judgmental inner voice that can tempt you to believe that nothing will help.
>
> - If you are in the open-minded group, you may tend to deny or be inattentive to feelings of anger or fear in yourself or others, and thereby ignore important issues. If you can focus on paying close attention to your experience and the experience of others, your balanced nature will help you find a fair and caring solution to the problem.

In this chapter you have seen that facing your fear of conflict is very important during stressful situations that may call for assertiveness. Self-reflection, watching out for false alarms from your mind and your sympathetic nervous system, and appreciating the strengths, hopes, needs, and flaws that you have in common with others will help you in this process. Looking at things as they are and trusting yourself and others takes courage, but when you exercise compassion toward everyone involved (including yourself), I believe you will find that the benefits are worth the discomfort. In the next chapter we will explore the last of the virtues that compassionate assertiveness emphasizes, and one of the most difficult to cultivate: forgiveness.

CHAPTER 6

Forgiveness: Free Yourself from Anger and Pain

Have you ever extended forgiveness to someone who has harmed you? Most likely, the answer is yes. But there probably have been other times when, for a variety of reasons, you have not been able or willing to forgive. What can help you forgive, and why should you, anyway? Before you try to cultivate forgiveness, you might want to know a little more about what forgiveness is and what it isn't.

What Is Forgiveness?

We all have an idea of what forgiveness is, but it is not an easy term to define. I think it is fair to say that forgiveness includes the ability to let go of hatred or wishes for revenge. At its highest level, forgiveness includes a willingness to consider that many causes and conditions, including pain or ignorance, can lead people to do bad things. But just as important as thinking about what forgiveness is, you should also consider what forgiveness is *not* (Enright 2001):

- Forgiveness is not glossing over wrongdoings, denying the seriousness of an offense, or pretending that things are different from the way they really are.

- Forgiveness is not excusing or condoning wrongdoing and does not remove appropriate consequences.

- Forgiveness does not mean you have to trust the person.

- Forgiveness does not have to involve reconciliation.

- Forgiveness is not denial or forgetting.

- Forgiveness is not an excuse to control other people.

Why It Can Be Hard to Forgive

As we all know, offering forgiveness is not always easy. When we have been hurt or betrayed, we are biologically primed by our neuroendocrine emergency responders to protect ourselves from further harm. Our reptilian brain and sympathetic nervous system instinctively prepare us to fight, flee, or freeze when we feel threatened; and in an effort to keep the negative experience from happening again, our amygdala and other parts of our limbic system often maintain our negative feelings—our anger, fear, or sorrow. Furthermore, the ruminating and judgmental part of our cerebral cortex can make it hard to let go of resentment and condemnation. This is even more true if the offense has been a serious one, or if the offender does not ask for forgiveness or express remorse. Therefore, it is understandable that forgiveness can take a great deal of inner strength.

Why Forgive?

Given that your self-protective instincts can make forgiveness difficult, it is legitimate to ask if it is worth it to forgive others for their hurtful actions. If forgiving takes so much work and courage, why bother? Is it any wonder that emotional wounds might make you want to wall yourself off from the people, activities, feelings, memories, and beliefs that make you feel vulnerable? Besides, why should you forgive people who hurt you? If they are bad, selfish, or mean, why should you care or worry about them? And what about justice's "eye for an eye" or extracting your "pound of flesh"? Isn't that fair?

In your heart you may sense that forgiveness and reconciliation will help you feel better, but fear, anger, or pride can get in the way. How can you trust that if you take a chance and extend forgiveness that you won't be humiliated or hurt again? Well, there is no guarantee, but in most cases forgiveness offers relief from suffering, can improve your relationships, and can bring you much more happiness and peace of mind than hatred and revenge will. But don't just take my word for it; look at the teachings of philosophy, ethics, and religion. The wisdom traditions with which I am familiar caution against the temptations of revenge and hatred. The "eye for an eye" instruction from the Bible, for example, which sounds brutal to us, was most likely an effort to promote justice over earlier tribal traditions of using extreme and excessive retaliation. Millions of people over the centuries have been inspired by the spiritual leaders of antiquity, such as Jesus and the Buddha, who encouraged mercy and forgiveness and urged us to let go of grudges and hatred, which not only hurt others but also interfere with our own moral and spiritual well-being. And let's not forget that the greatest leaders of modern times, including Desmond Tutu, Nelson Mandela, Mahatma Gandhi, the Dalai Lama, Martin Luther King, and Winston Churchill, were pressured to humiliate and seek vengeance against former enemies. Instead, they rejected hatred and chose reconciliation and forgiveness in order to heal their people and their countries.

The fields of psychology and peace studies have found that forgiveness can offer emotional healing as well, and many organizations have been founded in order to better understand forgiveness, as well as promote it. For example, Robert Enright, founder of the International Forgiveness Institute and author of *Forgiveness Is a Choice* (2001), has studied and written extensively on the topic of forgiveness. He has developed a twenty-step process of forgiveness that lays out in detail various aspects of forgiveness, including (1) acknowledging harm, (2) being willing to forgive, (3) experiencing empathy toward the offender, and (4) recognizing one's own mistakes that have required the forgiveness of others. Fred Luskin, founder of the Stanford University Forgiveness Project and author of *Forgive for Good: A Proven Prescription for Health and Happiness* (2002), offers ways to let go of anger and encourages us to choose forgiveness for our own benefit. And several studies funded by the Campaign for Forgiveness Research, a project supported by the John Templeton Foundation, have shown us that forgiveness helps decrease anger and depression and improve our day-to-day functioning. It even contributes to better health (Jones and Lawler 2001).

So consider that if you cling to hatred and self-righteousness, you may believe you have constructed a fortress that will keep you from feeling pain. But that fortress is like a house of cards: when you think about or are reminded of the person who hurt you, it can easily collapse and all those old feelings of helplessness, fear, anger, or confusion can come falling down around you. In fact, that's one of the most important points about forgiveness: you are not just doing it for the other person; ultimately you are doing it for yourself, because as long as hatred and bitterness reside within you, you are increasing your own suffering (Kornfield 2007).

○ *Mario's Story*

Mario came to me for help with anxiety and depression, which made it difficult for him to make reasonable requests of others, voice his opinion, and assert himself when appropriate. In telling me about his history, he described growing up in a family where his domineering mother continually berated his father, who was sweet and kind but also passive and detached. When Mario was seven years old his parents divorced and Mario went with his mother. His mother often criticized her ex-husband for not sending more money to support them, and Mario felt that at times she took out her frustration on him. He missed his father, with whom he had always felt very close, but unfortunately his father's visits became fewer and farther between. Increasingly doubting his father's love, Mario did not know how to keep the relationship going, especially since he sensed that his mother resented his previously close relationship with his father and he didn't want to upset her by pressing for more visits.

Mario lived with this wound even as an adult. He could not let go of his feelings of loss, anger, and anxiety. He could not forgive his mother for criticizing his father and "driving him away;" neither could he forgive his father for what Mario saw as abandoning him. Over the years, although he tried to numb himself to his pain, his hurt and anger continued to fester. Sometimes it focused on his mother, sometimes on his father, and sometimes on his sense of his own unworthiness, which he believed might have contributed on some level to his parents' divorce. His now elderly mother had mellowed over the years and his passive father had become more forthcoming, although they both retained their basic interpersonal styles. Mario tried to reconnect with and relate to both parents in a healthier way, but he still felt angry when he thought about his childhood and was on edge whenever he was around either of his parents. Underneath these feelings was the fact that he could not forgive them. He knew that his difficulty in forgiving his parents not only affected his ability to have a healthier relationship with his them, but also was affecting his life in other ways.

The Process of Forgiving

If you have decided to try to forgive another person, you have already started the journey. Next you need to have confidence that you can trust your own inner goodness and wisdom to guide your actions. Ask yourself, "What would I do if I were not afraid or angry?" Before you make a decision or act upon it, let the prefrontal part of your cerebral cortex help you recognize that hatred and bitterness work against your own well-being and that forgiveness will help you develop patience, equanimity, and the ability to stop the destructive cycle of negativity. Most people, in fact, acknowledge that revenge or retaliation has not brought them inner peace—in fact, it has generally made things worse.

To forgive, you must be willing to keep your heart open, even in the face of discomfort and uncertainty. This requires the courage to keep from instinctively cutting the person off, attacking him or her, or seeking revenge, and asks you to soften the part of your heart that you have hardened to keep from being hurt again.

At times people have told me that someone who hurt them is now "dead to them." Yet holding a grudge against that "dead" person can cause bitterness and suffering for years or even decades. Others have told me about times when they did something bad or made a big mistake and the other person forgave them and helped them do better. As a result, they were much more motivated to change than if the person they hurt had focused on punishing or humiliating them. Being forgiven had an added benefit as well: it made them more willing to forgive others when the shoe was on the other foot.

Barriers to Forgiveness

It is much easier to extend forgiveness when someone sincerely apologizes to us, whether or not we raise the issue. But what if, as in Mario's case, the other person doesn't ask for forgiveness? People who have hurt you may justify their behavior, or you may be afraid they will hurt you again if you forgive them. In these cases forgiveness can be especially difficult. But the main difficulty has to do with you and your ability to forgive someone in spite of these circumstances. In that case, as in Mario's situation, forgiveness requires an act of kindness and generosity and a determination to not let the other person's problems or mistakes ruin with your life.

Remember that forgiveness does not mean you should ignore wrongs, condone unacceptable behavior, or remove consequences. Indeed, forgiveness is "about healing the memory of the harm, not erasing it" (Alan 2006 128). Nor does it mean that you have to reconcile with or trust the other person if you believe that doing so may cause additional harm to you. In fact, it is in no one's best interest for you to maintain a relationship where you continue to be harmed. In such cases you may need to end the friendship, get a divorce, or find a new job.

When you are able to forgive, you are recognizing that the person who hurt you is a human being, just like you, with flaws and strengths, and that her misdeeds resulted from a variety of complex causes and conditions, many of which you may never even know about. Even if you never see or talk to her again, you can still keep your heart open and try to have compassion for her. Even if you need to protect yourself from future harm you can still acknowledge your common humanity with her and acknowledge that, like you, she has had suffering in her life. You might even find it in your heart to hope that someday she will be free from suffering and enjoy happiness. Besides the fact that it will ease your burden, if she is free from suffering and finds happiness she probably will no longer need to keep doing things that hurt others.

How the Four Principles of Compassionate Assertiveness Can Help You Forgive

In Mario's case, his anger toward his parents for their human flaws was holding him back from enjoying a good relationship with them or moving on with his life. Now let's see how the principles of compassionate assertiveness helped Mario free himself from his anger, hurt, and frustration, giving him the confidence to reach out to his parents while also setting appropriate limits with them and with other people as well.

Actions Are the Result of Complex Causes and Conditions

Mario began to think about the causes and conditions that led to his mother's hurtful behavior. He remembered that she was frustrated because his father was detached and unavailable for many household tasks and that his father avoided her by hiding behind a newspaper or in front of the TV. Mario remembered that his mother tried in vain to increase his father's involvement with him. And after the divorce, in addition to taking care of the house, Mario's mother, who had been out of the workforce for almost a decade, also had to shoulder most of the financial burdens. Was it any wonder that at times her anger boiled over?

Mario also began to recognize that his father, who worked long hours, was an introvert who needed quiet time for himself. Not able to assert himself with Mario's more outspoken and vocal mother, he withdrew more and more. After the divorce, Mario's father had his own financial struggles, and his ex-wife's complaints about money during his visits with Mario became more and more uncomfortable for him. Given these circumstances and his father's tendency to avoid conflict, Mario now saw that it was not surprising his father pulled away from him. Mario allowed himself to believe, however, that his father continued to love him in his own way.

This new perspective helped Mario think about his parents as people with challenges of their own but also see that their problems during those difficult years did not define them as human beings. It also helped him forgive his parents to admit to himself that he might not have done much better if he had been in their shoes.

Actions Have Consequences

Mario began to think about how the pressures of marriage, parenthood, and economic stress might have brought out irreconcilable differences between his parents that were not so apparent during their courtship.

He wondered if raising him contributed to their stress. Mario also wondered whether his mother or father ever wished that they had tried harder to make the marriage work.

As our work continued, Mario began to notice that his parents had grown over time. Although his mother had spoken badly of Mario's father for years, by now her criticism of him had almost completely disappeared, and she was also less critical of Mario. He also noticed that now, as an adult, on the occasions that he did see his father, his father was more relaxed and engaged than previously. Mario began to realize that he had spent many years looking at his parents through the lens of a young boy. He also was beginning to see that, just as he had grown and changed over the years, so had his parents, and he considered the possibility that maybe they had learned some valuable life lessons from both their marriage and their divorce.

Intentions Matter

Looking back, it occurred to Mario that for all their flaws and limitations, in their own ways his parents had both intended to be there for him, both before and after the divorce. As his own memories began to expand to include the positives, he remembered that before the divorce his dad used to take him on walks and read him bedtime stories, which allowed them quiet time together, and how after the divorce his father tried, especially at the beginning, to stay connected with him. He also remembered how before and after the divorce his mother made his lunch, helped him with his homework, and took him to the park, and after the divorce she showed tremendous strength and determination in taking care of her son as best she could.

Follow the Middle Way

Thinking about these things helped soften Mario's heart toward both of his parents. He was able to recognize that, just like him, neither parent was completely right or wrong, or entirely good or bad. Looking at the big picture, he also realized that he had been dwelling in the past, and both he and his parents were now older and wiser. He now saw that they had mellowed and, to a large degree, moved on and that he could do so as well. Mario began to think about ways he could use compassionate assertiveness to set limits with his domineering mother and to reach out more to his introverted father. He would try to let go of his anger while also working on asserting himself with his parents and with others as well.

Asking for Forgiveness from Others

Let's face it: At one time or another we have all harmed or neglected another person, intentionally or unintentionally. Compassionate assertiveness includes our willingness to ask for forgiveness as well as to extend it to others. Just as forgiving someone takes courage, so does expressing genuine regret and remorse for a hurtful act you have committed.

"But," you may reply, "asking for forgiveness makes me vulnerable to possible humiliation by the other person. What if he refuses to forgive me? What if he uses the opportunity to 'rub it in'?"

These "what ifs" are just as applicable as the difficulties described when we talked about forgiving others. And once again, it all boils down to your willingness to look at the truth as it really is, with courage and an open heart. The experience of asking for forgiveness is a reminder that we all make mistakes, and by taking responsibility for yours, you can resolve problems in a way that you never could by denial or pride. It is much easier for someone to forgive you if you apologize in a sincere and openhearted manner than if you try to convince him that you were in the right. Sometimes, too, we can fool ourselves into thinking we are apologizing when we really aren't. How familiar does this false apology sound: "I'm sorry I…, but it was your fault because…"? You may resist taking responsibility in order to save your pride and dignity, but this false refuge can actually prevent the other person from being able to forgive you.

It's just as important to ask forgiveness for sins of omission as sins of commission. Sins of omission can include letting someone down by not keeping a promise or neglecting to be responsive to a call for help. These also include not offering help when you know someone needs it, including standing by when someone is hurting another person, as in bullying or abusive situations. Since intervening in some way may make you a target of aggression, it is an act of bravery and one we don't always have the strength to take. As hard as it might be to apologize for not having helped someone in a time of need, there is good reason to do so if you are able, not only for the other person's benefit, but also for your own peace of mind. Statements like "I know I should have done better" or "I didn't have the maturity or strength to help at the time, and for that I am so sorry" can go a long way in making things right.

But asking for forgiveness is only part of the story. In addition, it is important to take responsibility for your mistakes by committing yourself to do better in the future and making amends to the person as best you can. So asking for forgiveness should not be just a verbal exercise where you say "I'm sorry" and get off the hook. It also involves an effort to make things right by accepting responsibility and finding out what you can do to make it up to the person you have wronged (Tabak et al. 2012). If you borrowed a book from someone and lost it, you can purchase a gift certificate for a bookstore, or you can offer to replace the book or pay for a different one. If you forgot your offer to help someone move on a particular day and didn't show up, you can ask if you can make it up to him in some way, like taking him out to dinner or helping him unpack or paint. Sometimes you might not know how to show your remorse. In that case you can say, "I know I let you down and I can't undo the past. Please tell me what I can do to make it up to you," and see what the person says. Don't assume that if you do not ask for forgiveness the other person will not notice the transgression or will forget about it. Even if the person never says anything to you, most likely he will feel wounded and his trust in you will be compromised.

But what if the person is not willing to accept your apology or allow you to make amends? What if he says it is "too little, too late" and stops trusting you or even ends the relationship? If you have really made an effort, then you need to accept the consequences of your actions and try to learn from your mistake. This may be a painful experience, but you must also accept the fact that we cannot force anyone to forgive, nor do we have the power to control the thoughts, feelings, or (ultimately) the behavior of anyone else.

In the Jewish tradition, if you sincerely apologize to someone you have harmed and try to rectify the wrongdoing, the wronged individual is ethically bound to extend forgiveness. And just in case it slipped your mind to ask, forgiveness comes to the forefront between the High Holidays of Rosh Hashanah and Yom Kippur. During that time, Jewish people throughout the world reach out to others to apologize and even ask if they have hurt others or treated them unfairly and, if so, whether there is anything they can do to make amends. If the other person forgives, then both individuals can start the Jewish New Year with a clean slate and a healed heart. And if the person still will not forgive? Then, after three attempts to express genuine remorse and make amends, the sin of wrongdoing is shifted to him. I think this tradition would be a good one for all of us to adopt on a day-to-day basis.

Forgiving Yourself

Sometimes we are our own harshest critics when we think about the hurtful things we have done to ourselves and others. When you cause others pain—whether you are speaking unkind words during an argument, gossiping about a friend, lashing out at a relative, or humiliating a coworker—it is a good thing to recognize this and to feel the sting of remorse, because this first-arrow kind of pain is a signal to offer an apology and make amends if possible. But if you take this self-criticism to an extreme by second-arrow condemnation of yourself as a worthless person, it can actually get in the way of making things right. I regret not having been more attentive and appreciative to my wonderful grandparents, who were very generous and forgiving and who always gave me love and support. They are all deceased now, so I can't apologize to them in person. But I try to honor their memory by attempting to be the kind of person they would have been proud of. And I try to forgive myself, remembering that in my youth I did not have the maturity and good sense to recognize and fulfill my responsibilities to them. I also have encouraged my own children to learn from my mistakes—to keep in touch with their grandparents and to show gratitude for all of their acts of kindness and generosity.

Later in our work, Mario admitted regret that as a child he had not worked harder to keep in touch with his father and had not let his mother know how hard it was on him to be used as a sounding board for her negative thoughts and feelings. However, he came to realize that he had been just a child at the time and that it is difficult for most children to show initiative of that kind. This helped him forgive himself and his parents for their human flaws and recognize that the past was over and he could move on with his life.

When you face your own missteps with a compassionate heart, you can remind yourself that mistakes and weaknesses are human tendencies and not signs of a fatally flawed individual. In fact, true self-forgiveness is an acknowledgment of the very human flaws each and every one of us has—flaws that remind us of the work that is needed to meet our potential and that help us humbly acknowledge our bonds with the other imperfect beings on this earth. Like other forms of forgiveness, this kind of work takes courage, because it requires that we look deep into our heart at the dark side of the human experience with honesty and compassion. But the rewards of self-forgiveness are much greater than the pain of looking within. By doing so we increase our ability to empathize and identify with others, deepen our peace of mind, and gain freedom from the debilitating power of hatred or self-loathing (Kornfield 2007).

An Invitation: Contemplate Forgiveness

Allow yourself to think about a time when someone hurt you, either intentionally or unintentionally. Are you willing to consider that there were causes and conditions that might have led to her behavior? Can you consider that her intention may not have been to harm you, but even if it was, not take it too personally, but rather see her actions as the result of a variety of causes and conditions? See if you can be upset with what she did without condemning her as a person. Perhaps you can find the strength to soften your heart and recognize that you, too, have done hurtful things in the past that have required forgiveness. And even if you will never see the person again, see if you can genuinely hope that someday she may be free from suffering and find genuine happiness.

Now think of a time when you hurt another person, intentionally or unintentionally. Can you picture yourself recognizing the reality of what you did and acknowledging the causes and conditions that led you to that place? Contemplate what your intentions were. Imagine yourself asking that person for forgiveness. See if you can think of ways to take responsibility for your mistake and do what is needed to make things right. And if the other person cannot find it in his heart to forgive you for your mistakes, see if you can forgive him for not being able to forgive you.

Now see if you can forgive yourself for harming yourself or another because of fear, ignorance, or anger, acknowledging that human mistakes are inevitable. Commit to doing your best to take responsibility for repairing any harm you have done and to doing better in the future.

Finally, feel your kinship with the people you encounter each day, all of whom at some time or another have harmed or been harmed by others. Now make a wish that they, and you, may be free from suffering and the causes of suffering—and that all may enjoy happiness and the causes of happiness.

Consider the Implications for Your Interpersonal Style

What are the unique strengths and challenges you bring to the task of forgiveness?

- If you are in the enthusiastic group, your willingness to forgive is one of your strengths. Your challenge may be to refrain from trying to control the feelings of others.

- If you are in the discerning group, your strength will be in your willingness to see the truth when matters of forgiveness arise. Your greatest difficulty, though, may be your tendency to be overly critical of yourself or others, thereby creating barriers to forgiveness.

- If you are in the open-minded group, your strength may lie in your capacity to understand the complexity of the causes and conditions that lead to mistakes and misdeeds. Your challenge may be pushing yourself to make that extra effort by attending to your feelings and those of others so that true healing and reconciliation can take place.

In this chapter we have explored forgiveness and how practicing it can affect you and the people in your life. I hope you have come to see that forgiveness can help you heal, give you peace of mind, and allow you to develop the full, rich relationships that you deserve.

Having completed the four chapters in this part of the book, you are now familiar with how gratitude, equanimity, courage, and forgiveness can help you use compassionate assertiveness in your life. In part 3 we will put these inner strengths into action by exploring mindfulness/meditation, communication, and negotiation skills, the rest of the tools you will need to master compassionate assertiveness. If you are ready, it's time to take the next step.

PART 3

Strengthening Your Interpersonal Skills

CHAPTER 7

Using Mindfulness and Meditation to Calm Your Body and Your Mind

Earlier in this book, we examined how your neuroendocrine emergency responder system, the guardian of your physical safety and well-being, can misinterpret events and unduly influence you to regard others as threatening, resulting in self-protective but often misguided reactions, such as the fight, flight, or freeze response. We also saw how cultivating certain virtues—gratitude, equanimity, courage, and forgiveness—can help you understand and work with the difficult emotions of anger, fear, and confusion when interpersonal problems arise. But reading and thinking about these virtues is not enough. In order to live what you have learned, you need to actually practice the "how" of compassionate assertiveness.

The next step in the process involves creating a link between the values that you have already learned about, and improving certain interpersonal skills, which you will be reading about in the next two chapters. In this chapter, we will explore ways for you to manage the problematic sensations, thoughts, and emotions that can occur in times of interpersonal stress, which will provide that link. The techniques involve integrating the mental process of concentration and reflection with the physical process of mobilizing your parasympathetic nervous system to calm your body and your mind. The skills that constitute that link are *mindfulness* and *meditation*.

Mindfulness: What It Is and How It Can Help

Mindfulness is a way of being attentive to your thoughts, emotions, and bodily sensations without being judgmental. It can be used as a "stand-alone" technique or incorporated into a meditation practice. Mindfulness is sometimes referred to as having two "wings": awareness and compassion (Brach 2003, 26–28).

The First Wing of Mindfulness

The first wing of mindfulness involves acknowledging the sensations, thoughts, beliefs, and feelings that you are experiencing at a given moment. You don't have to like or agree with what comes to mind; the goal is to simply acknowledge your inner experiences.

Let's say that someone bumps into you at a party and spills his drink on you. If he is a close friend, you may laugh about it together, believing that it was a silly accident that could happen to anyone; in fact, it might occur to you that it may have been you who bumped into him. So your thoughts, feelings, and reactions are playful and relaxed. But let's say that the person is a stranger. In that case, you might be mildly irritated and believe that the other person is clumsy or careless. And if he is someone you very much dislike, you may believe that he actually spilled his drink on you on purpose. In that case you could feel very angry.

The external reality is that someone spilled his drink on you. But if you are being mindful, you are aware that at that moment you feel relaxed, irritated, or angry and that you are making assumptions based on your beliefs about his intentions. But you may not be aware that those assumptions and beliefs might not be true. As you use mindfulness to work with your feelings and beliefs, you begin to experience your mental processes with more clarity, and might even begin to consider granting someone you don't like the same benefit of the doubt you would give to someone you really care about. This mental shift can be such a powerful experience that it can actually transform your attitudes and actions.

In my own experience, when I have been aware of jumping to negative conclusions I generally have felt embarrassed or ashamed of myself. It's the kind of feeling that can scare any of us away from being really honest with ourselves; after all, it isn't always easy to face our shortcomings. Certainly, I don't like to think of myself as having suspicious or judgmental moments, but when I am truly honest with myself, I can see that they do crop up from time to time. This is why the willingness to be in contact with your own inner experiences, whether in the moment or upon later reflection, can be so difficult. In fact, it can be so hard that in the Buddhist tradition those who walk this path are sometimes referred to as spiritual warriors. So what can you do to give yourself the strength to stand up to the false refuge of denial or illusions about yourself or others? Fortunately, compassion, the second wing of mindfulness, is there to help.

The Second Wing of Mindfulness

The second wing of mindfulness is compassion, that inborn quality of deep caring and a wish that all beings might be free from suffering and the causes of suffering. However, as we know, it is not always easy to access the compassion within us, especially when we become caught up in our own fear, anger, confusion, or ego. Therefore in mindful awareness, in addition to seeking truth at each moment, we also seek the ability to arouse feelings of compassion toward ourselves and others, through such thoughts as "I care about your suffering" or "I forgive." This level of compassion goes even deeper than words; it is a heartfelt and gentle effort to heal a tender emotional wound.

The Lotus Blossom

A metaphor for mindfulness as a path to awakening is that of the lotus blossom. The red lotus is especially relevant to our cultivation of compassionate assertiveness because it symbolizes the pure nature of the heart and represents compassion and love in its many forms.

The lotus begins its life as a seed within a pod, nestled in a muddy bed under still water in a pond or lake. It can lie there, dormant, for many years, waiting until conditions are just right for it to grow. At that point, the emerging plant forces the pod open and sets its roots in the mud. As its strong stem grows, it pushes upward until it finally breaks the water's surface, its pristine petals opening in the warmth and glow of the morning sun.

Like the flowering of the lotus, personal growth is also a transformational process. It is difficult to break out of the self-protective armor that binds us, to acknowledge and understand the "mud"—the inner and outer causes and conditions that both cause suffering and give us the nourishment to overcome it—and to baptize ourselves with awareness and honesty. But although you will be taking some emotional risks, I hope you will trust that cultivating the virtues we have already explored and dedicating time to learn the contemplative skills of mindfulness and meditation will lead to increased inner peace and healthier relationships.

What Mindfulness Helps You Remember

The two wings of mindfulness—awareness and compassion—help you cultivate inner strength by reminding you that:

- It is inevitable that you will experience a certain amount of pain in your life, some of which you create for yourself (second-arrow suffering).

- There is, has always been, and will always be, goodness within you.

- Intentions matter.

- Your mistakes and vulnerabilities do not define you.

- Your interpersonal difficulties are a result of causes and conditions.

- Once you are aware of causes and conditions, new causes and conditions are created, which you can act upon to benefit yourself and others.

- Taking responsibility and accepting the consequences of your mistakes and weaknesses are valuable learning experiences.

o Every moment is a fresh moment and a new learning opportunity.

o You can choose the freedom of short-term discomfort and long-term peace over short-term gratification and long-term suffering.

In other words, as you face the discomfort of honest reflection regarding your thoughts, feelings, behavior, and intentions, you can give yourself a break and treat yourself to the same level of understanding and kindness that you would afford to the most beloved person in your life. And this has another purpose as well: it will remind you to extend the same patience and understanding that you offer to the people you love to others you encounter every day.

Meditation

Meditation is a time-honored practice of looking inward to cultivate inner strength. It is a training ground for developing concentration, relaxation, and mindfulness and for contemplating various virtues, including those we have discussed. But is it possible that setting aside twenty minutes to meditate three or four times a week can actually help you sharpen your mind, stay calm in the face of adversity, open your heart, and improve your relationships?

A growing number of scientific studies have provided evidence that this is the case. They have shown that meditation can change the structure of your brain (Hölzel et al. 2011; Lazar et al. 2005); help your brain process information more efficiently (Slagter et al. 2007); decrease emotional reactivity (Creswell et al. 2007); help you cope with stress (Nidich et al. 2009); and increase empathy (Lutz et al. 2008). These studies demonstrate that meditation, which has been around for more than two thousand years, may benefit you in ways that psychologists are just beginning to appreciate.

The Practice of Meditation

When you think of meditation, you might conjure up an image of someone wearing a monk's robe and sitting in a cross-legged position in a candle-lit temple. While the benefits of meditation may be more easily obtained by practicing it in a rarified setting, such a setting is not necessary (Young 2002). Meditation can be practiced anywhere, and I have meditated in places as unlikely as a subway train. Most often, though, it helps for you to be in a quiet location where you won't be distracted or interrupted, one that lets you focus on your meditation practice. Sitting on the floor or in a chair in an uncluttered setting and wearing comfortable clothing is helpful. The meditation process described below includes concentration, mindfulness, and contemplation, but meditation can also be practiced with a focus on only one or two of these.

Concentration. As you settle in, you may want to begin with an aspiration for what you would like to accomplish during the meditation session (for example, "May I be at peace"). If you prefer, you can state it as something you have already accomplished ("I am at peace").

The initial focus of meditation is usually on the breath, but you can also listen to the sounds around you or to a recorded chant or instructor's voice. A good compromise can be to breathe in such a way that you can actually hear the sound of your own breath; this involves a slight tightening of the muscles in the back of the upper area of the throat and is sometimes called "ocean breathing."

One breathing technique involves simply observing your own breath. Another technique involves slow, deep breathing, with each full in- and out-breath cycle taking about ten seconds, resulting in six complete cycles per minute, much slower than the average of fourteen to sixteen cycles per minute. Slow, deep breathing mobilizes the parasympathetic nervous system, which can help your mind become receptive and your body relaxed. Some people focus on doing just this form of meditation, developing their concentration skills by finding a single point of focus and staying with it.

One interesting aspect of this kind of experience is noticing how your "monkey mind" (the tendency of the mind to jump from thought to thought, just as a monkey jumps from branch to branch, and from tree to tree) tempts you away from the intended object of your attention. This is perfectly normal, and one of the main purposes of this form of meditation is to observe that you are distracted and then return your focus to your breath (or to sounds) (Salzberg 2011). Many people find that when this happens it is helpful to use such techniques as counting breaths or thinking the words "in" on the in-breath and "out" on the out-breath, to keep them anchored (Thich Nhat Hanh 1990).

As you slowly tame your mind, you will increase your ability to bring your body and mind into a state that is both relaxed and alert, the ideal state for working with interpersonal difficulties.

Mindfulness. As mentioned earlier in this chapter, mindfulness does not have to be practiced as part of a meditation exercise, but it often is. Here you bring your awareness to your various bodily and sensory experiences, thoughts, beliefs, and emotions and observe how they change moment by moment during the meditation exercise. During this time you can use the first wing of mindfulness to focus on your immediate experience rather than on the external events that produced it or on judgments about yourself or others. For example, in mindfulness, instead of dwelling on such thoughts as "He took advantage of me; what an idiot I was to allow it," you might think "Right now I am feeling angry (or hurt, or regret)."

In the quiet, inward experience of mindfulness meditation, you are aware of the flow of sensations, thoughts, beliefs, and emotions you are experiencing at the moment, examining them as best you can with honesty and curiosity (Kabat-Zinn 1990). It is as if you are on the bank of a river watching leaves float by—observing them in an interested way, without judging them as good or bad. Your train of thought might be something like this: "At this moment [or "right now"] I am aware that I am [describe your immediate experience]…thinking/worrying/anticipating/remembering/feeling anger/feeling tightness in my neck/back/stomach/chest." Or you can give yourself a little more distance from potentially overwhelming thoughts or feelings by using such phrases as "Regret is present" rather than "I am feeling regret." Beliefs can be explored too. "Right now I believe that I am unworthy…" and then allow yourself to explore that belief in a gentle manner.

It is sometimes helpful to label your experience in the present moment as "pleasant," "unpleasant," or "neutral." This is different from judging it: you are just recognizing what your response is at that moment and how it is affecting you right then and there. Accept the presence of even unpleasant thoughts and feelings. You can ask yourself, "What is this?" and investigate whatever comes up, noticing when it changes or is replaced with another thought or feeling. This is sometimes referred to as "beginner's mind" (Batchelor 2009). By the way, if you feel that the meditation session is not going as well as you would like, join the club! Even very experienced meditators encounter this, and you can use your feelings about it as well: "I am avoiding looking at this," "I am judging myself/him," or "I am feeling confused/bored."

While you are noticing your sensations, thoughts, beliefs, and feelings, try to bring in the second wing of compassion by holding your observations in a caring and patient manner. As best you can, try to refrain from judging yourself for having thoughts or feelings that you feel ashamed of or embarrassed to admit, even to yourself, and be gentle with yourself if you feel that your meditation is not going as well as you had hoped. If you find yourself judging yourself (or others) or feeling that your mistakes or flaws define you as a person, you can use compassionate thoughts about yourself, just as you might with a dear relative or friend, to help you find a balanced perspective. If you feel overwhelmed you can take a "break" by shifting your awareness back to your breath or to sounds around you as safe harbors to calm you down, and if you wish to, you can return to mindfulness meditation after a little while.

Contemplation. As with mindfulness, contemplative meditation can be practiced in day-to-day life or as part of a meditation exercise on its own or combined with concentration and/or mindfulness. Contemplative meditation, such as the meditation on gratitude in chapter 3, generally involves focusing on a specific virtue with the intention of strengthening it (Kornfield 2007). Some common contemplative meditation practices are on compassion—the wish for freedom from the causes of suffering, including our human tendency toward grasping, hatred, and delusion—and loving-kindness, the deep desire for happiness and the causes of happiness, for ourselves and others. In general, this kind of meditation begins with yourself and is then expanded to others, being as specific as you can and even using visualization. Here is an example:

May I (or others) be free of suffering and the causes of suffering.

May I (or others) enjoy happiness and the causes of happiness.

May I (or others) be safe from inner and outer harm.

May I (or others) be at peace.

What if you think you "should" feel a certain way but you don't? Even if the sentiments don't feel meaningful to you, it can still benefit you to "try on" the concepts and see what happens after practicing the meditation several times. And if you can't bring yourself to do that much, then you can meditate on that, using gentle messages, such as "Forgiveness is more than I can manage right now" or "I will send compassion to this person when I am ready." With contemplation meditation you can always begin just where you are.

As you can imagine, these practices are often easier said than done, but they become more manageable with repetition. Let's now see how meditation skills can be applied to compassionate assertiveness.

○ *Emily's Story*

Emily was dating Richard, a sweet, generous, and intelligent man. She liked him a lot and they had fun with each other. Emily had a great deal of respect and affection for Richard, and he seemed to feel the same way about her when they were together.

However, Emily was frustrated that Richard rarely initiated phone calls or came up with ideas about where to go or what to do when they were together. It seemed to her that she was doing too much of the work in the relationship, and she was starting to resent it. At the same time, she was afraid to talk to Richard about it, thinking that he might break up with her if she upset him or rocked the boat.

With my assistance, Emily began to meditate on this dilemma, first calming her body and mind using slow, deep breaths, which helped her relax and focus on her immediate sensory experience. She then expanded and shifted her focus to her thoughts, feelings, and sensations. The first thoughts that came up were that Richard was too passive for her and that he was also irresponsible for not initiating contacts. Then she caught herself…and became aware that she was focusing on him, not on her own experiences at that moment. And what were those experiences? She got on track by redirecting her awareness to her immediate internal experience. "Right now I am aware that I am judging him." Then, "At this moment I am aware that anger is present…" As she allowed herself to investigate the beliefs associated with anger, she had another realization: "At this moment I am aware that I believe that he should be able to read my mind and know what I want. Right now I am feeling embarrassed about that. My embarrassment is unpleasant to me." Next she thought, "Right now, I feel tightness in my chest" and then "Right now I am aware that fear is present because I don't want him to break up with me and think he might."

Emily stayed with this for a while, then spontaneously some wisdom bubbled up. "At this moment I believe that if I don't address this problem things may only get worse," she said, and then "Right now I feel a desire to talk about my concerns with him so I can adjust my expectations or accept that the relationship isn't right for me." She checked in with her body and noticed that even though she didn't know the outcome of a discussion with Richard, her chest felt less constricted, and some of the tension and weight she had been carrying was easing. "Right now, I believe that I can speak up and be open to whatever happens," she observed. "How does that feel to you right now?" I asked her. "Calmer," she replied.

Emily then moved to contemplative meditation. She got in touch with feelings of loving-kindness toward Richard. She allowed herself to be aware of the many qualities in him that she valued. This helped her think about him in a less critical way. Whether or not things worked out between them, she now thought, she felt compassion and unconditional friendliness toward him. She thought about her own anger and her worries, noting that these feelings were focused on thoughts about the past and the future, instead of the present moment. She then brought up the following wish: "May I be free from inner and outer harm. May I be free from suffering and the causes of suffering. May I enjoy happiness and the causes of happiness. May I be at peace."

She then pictured Richard in her mind and said, "May you be free from inner and outer harm. May you be free from suffering and the causes of suffering. May you enjoy happiness and the causes of happiness. May you be at peace." As she sat there, Emily now rested in the awareness that she could address her concerns with Richard with much less anger and fear, and she ended the meditation session in a much calmer state than when she began.

An Invitation: Explore Meditation and Mindfulness

For meditation and mindfulness to help you in your day-to-day life you need to do it on a regular basis, not just when you are upset with someone. In this way, you are "sharpening the ax" (Young 2002) so that you will be prepared for events that could cause your neuroendocrine system's emergency responders and your negative thoughts to overwhelm you. As you become more skilled at meditative techniques, the skills you learn will arise more naturally in your everyday experience.

Find a quiet space and a regular time to meditate. Sit quietly in an upright but comfortable position, in a chair or on a cushion, with your knees lower than your hips. Using flowers or a lit candle as an "entering" point will set the mood for this exercise but is not necessary. After a few moments of settling in, you may want to close your eyes. Some people enjoy listening to audio recordings with "meditation" instructions music, or chanting. If you decide to try that, just notice whether it is distracting to you or if you become overly dependent on it; if so, you may want to decrease or eliminate your use of it.

Now you are ready to begin reading the following meditation script, which should take about fifteen minutes. If possible, record it so that later you can listen to it rather than read it. Modify it in any way that is helpful for you.

Take a few slow, deep breaths, and if you desire to do so close your eyes, to help you enter into a state of relaxed but alert presence. Draw your attention to your sensations—the sounds around you, the sound of your breath, your physical sensations related to sitting at this moment. As you draw inward, contemplate what you would like to gain from this meditation session today. Is your intention to be healed, to be at peace, to gain wisdom or understanding, or to increase your happiness? Set your aspiration. Practice thinking about it as already being true—for example, "Happiness is present"—and see how that feels to you.

[Pause 1–2 minutes]

Now draw your mind to a sensory focal point that will serve as your anchor. Perhaps it is your breath. If so, notice the rise and fall of your chest or belly with each in-breath and out-breath. Or notice the sensation as cool air enters and is released through your nostrils. Or perhaps you prefer to listen to the sounds around you. [Pause] Your mind will want to pull you away from your focus. Notice when you are "somewhere else," and as best you can, return your attention to your object of concentration. You are training your mind, disciplining it to hold attention on what you choose to focus on and to observe what is there, without judging, moment by moment.

[Pause 2–3 minutes. Periodically say, "And when your mind wanders, gently but firmly lead it back. You can always think about those other things later."]

Next we will shift to the mindfulness part of the meditation. Notice any thoughts, beliefs, images, feelings, or sensations that move through your field of awareness. Your emphasis is not only on what arises, but also on your awareness of awareness. "Right now I am aware…" Watch the stream of experience as it flows through your mind. Notice the interplay between awareness of thoughts and beliefs and how they interact with your emotions and sensation.

[Pause 2–3 minutes, periodically saying, "And if your mind wanders, just bring it back to the present moment."]

Investigate the experience with words, such as "What is this?" If you are disturbed by what comes up, examine it gently. Allow yourself to recognize your own vulnerabilities, mistakes, and missteps, while giving yourself and others the benefit of the doubt. Remember that whatever arises is impermanent and does not define you. It is a fleeting experience that reflects that moment. It is a result of complex causes and conditions that may obscure but never destroy the goodness within you that is part of your authentic ground of being and is a reminder that each moment is unique.

[Pause 1–2 minutes]

Finally, send a message of compassion, loving-kindness, forgiveness, or gratitude to yourself, a loved one, someone you feel neutral about, or, if you are ready, even someone you have negative feelings toward. Or, if you wish, you can send an aspiration that includes a general message of love and care to yourself or others—for example:

May I be free of suffering and the causes of suffering.
May I enjoy happiness and the causes of happiness.
May I be safe from inner and outer harm.
May I be at peace.

As you send this same caring message outward, allow yourself to be receptive to loving thoughts and feelings that are being sent your way by people who

care about you, or maybe even people all over the world, people you don't even know, who are sending messages of love and caring to all beings, including you.
[Pause 1–2 minutes]
Now return to the aspiration you evoked when you started this exercise. Repeat it to yourself, this time using present-tense language, as if your wish has been granted. See how that feels to you. And when you are ready, take a few more deep, slow breaths, open your eyes, and take the comfort and awareness that you feel at this moment with you as you go on with your day.

Consider the Implications for Your Interpersonal Style

- If you have an enthusiastic interpersonal style, it may help you to include a focus on awareness of the transitory nature or negative aspects of things that you desire. This will help you let go of grasping.

- If you have a discerning interpersonal style, it may help you to include a focus on loving-kindness in your meditation practice. This will help you let go of anger and judging.

- If you have an open-minded interpersonal style, it may help you to meditate on your breath or on sounds. This will help you discipline your mind and help you focus.

In this chapter you have learned about your mind-body connection and how you can develop meditative skills—concentration, relaxation, mindfulness, and contemplation of virtues—to access the compassion, wisdom, and equanimity you already possess. In the next chapter we focus on improving your communication skills—one of two interpersonal tools that will complete your compassionate assertiveness tool kit.

CHAPTER 8

Communicating with Care: How to Understand and Be Understood

You have begun to expand your perspective and cultivate heartfelt concern for yourself and others, and you have also found out a bit about how to calm your body and clear your mind. But as any dancer can tell you, you can learn the steps to a waltz by yourself, but until you practice with a partner you can never master the dance. This applies to compassionate assertiveness as well, as we will see when we delve into two important interpersonal tools in this chapter and the next: caring communication and thoughtful negotiation.

In this chapter we will focus on communication skills. Here you will learn how to avoid misunderstandings and how to express your feelings and needs in a clear and caring way. You will also learn how to respond wisely when you are on the receiving end of a concern or request. In many situations, just the expression of concern by you or the other person may well be enough to solve the problem. These are circumstances where, once you understand each other's feelings and needs, you and the other person will be able to have a meeting of the minds.

Communication: There's More to It Than Meets the Ear

Communication occurs in a social context, one that requires us to apply old learning to new situations. During any interaction, your brain automatically tries to find ways to apply what you have learned so that you can communicate easily and effectively.

This is especially true when there has been a pattern of hurt or frustration. If you are expecting problems because of past experiences, then you may be inclined to believe the worst of people and make negative assumptions about their intentions and behavior. Those negative thoughts can cloud your understanding of the reality of a situation, as well as influence your verbal and behavioral communications, making a difficult situation even more difficult. At the very least, miscommunication and negative assumptions can create confusion or unwarranted suspicion between two well-meaning people. At worst, they can end relationships, create enemies, fuel prejudice, and even lead to violence.

An Invitation: Interpreting the Actions of Others

Think about a situation when you were upset, hurt, or annoyed about something someone said or did (or didn't do) and later found out that because you did not know the whole story, you had misinterpreted or misunderstood the situation. What did you believe, feel, say, or do before you discovered the truth? How did you feel when you discovered that you had misinterpreted the situation? Looking back on it now, what, if anything, do you wish you had done differently?

Bringing Compassionate Assertiveness into Your Communication with Others

Compassionate assertiveness involves expressing your concerns, needs, and requests, for your own welfare and for the welfare of the other person. This is not always easy to do, especially if confusion, anger, or fear interfere with clear thinking or cause you to harden your heart. However, since compassionate assertiveness is a skill that can be accessed using the strength and wisdom already within you, with a little knowledge and practice this kind of communication will become easier and easier. Here are some principles to keep in mind when you prepare to address a concern or to make a request using the compassionate assertiveness approach:

- Get in touch with the positives, cultivate patience, and calm your mind and body. Keep causes and conditions in mind with regard to both you and the other person.

- Let the Golden Rule guide you. Think about what you would want someone to say to you if she was upset with you for some reason.

- Try to assume benign or at least neutral intentions on the other person's part.

- Remember that your intentions and the emotions that drive them will affect your actions and that your actions will have consequences. So try to think about what you would do if you were not afraid or angry. That can guide you to a response that reflects both wisdom and a caring heart.

- Stay on the path of the middle way. There is no need to be either a doormat or a tyrant.

The Process of Communicating Using Compassionate Assertiveness

Whenever we interact with another person we communicate not only with our words, but also with our body language and facial expressions. The pacing, timing, and sequencing of what you say and how you say it can also influence how the message is received. In this section we will explore how compassionate assertiveness can make a positive contribution to the process. Be aware that the sequencing and wording described below may not be right for you in every situation. Your good intentions will be your best guide in the process—think of them as your north star in deciding your course of action.

Initiating a Conversation

To initiate a discussion about a concern, approach the other person when you are calm and there is enough time and privacy to fully explore the topic. When approaching the person, try to use a tone of voice and choice of words that show that you are seeking to grasp the whole picture. Try to maintain an attitude of friendliness and your body language will follow suit.

Emphasize what you have actually observed, or ask a question in a neutral way. Statements or questions like "I noticed…" "When I came home…" "Do you remember when…" or "Have you noticed…?" can be helpful in introducing the topic. Try to be specific—for instance, "I noticed that the door was left unlocked last night" rather than "You always leave the door unlocked."

Try to avoid questions that could come across as accusatory or aggressive. For instance, "I can't find my brush; have you seen it?" is preferable to the accusatory "What did you do with my brush?" Even a simple and nonjudgmental "What happened?" can open up a door to understanding a situation that may or may not be a problem. Remember that you may not know the whole story, so try to resist jumping to potentially faulty conclusions about what happened or about the other person's intentions.

Engaging in a Dialogue

Allow plenty of space for the other person to respond. Check in with him by soliciting his perspective ("Is that how you see it?" "Do you think I am seeing this clearly?"). The old saying, "Seek first to understand, then to be understood," and my grandmother's adage that "we have two ears and only one mouth" remind us that listening with care is the foundation of healthy communication.

Try to communicate that you assume the other person's good intentions ("You may not be aware..." or "I'm sure that you meant well..."). Phrases like "you didn't bother to..." or "you didn't want me to..." ascribe negative intentions to the other person and should be avoided because they are likely to result in a hostile response (think about how you would feel if someone said those things to you).

It is tempting to overstate your case by using exaggerated comments that include words like "always" and "never," but these usually put people on the defensive. As hard as it might be when you are feeling very critical, try to understate rather than overstate, using "on occasion..." or "I've noticed that the past few times...." to soften the criticism and allow the other person to stay open to your concern. This approach shows that you see the problems as exceptions rather than the rule, even if at the moment it doesn't feel that way.

Self-disclosure that includes sensitivity to the other person's feelings can also show your intention to strengthen the relationship. Some examples are "This isn't easy for me to bring up, but..." and "I'm feeling uncomfortable with..." In addition, it will work to your benefit to show humility and to acknowledge the possibility that you may have contributed to the problem ("I don't think I discussed this with you before..." or "I realize that I may have confused you when I...").

Sharing Your Feelings

Sometimes a problem is resolved just by stating an observation. For instance, if you say, "We haven't gone out for the evening in over a month," and the other person says, "That's true. Let's do something this weekend," then the problem is solved. But if the person is unresponsive or dismisses your concern (for instance, "I don't like going out"), it is probably time to express your feelings and needs.

Compassionate assertiveness includes expressing your feelings in a way that is open and conciliatory rather than aggressive or hostile. You can express your feelings using words like "frustrated," "worried," "concerned," "demoralized," "uncomfortable," "embarrassed," or "humiliated" and phrases like "When you walked away I felt so frustrated." Try to resist the temptation to use "I feel" as a prelude to an accusation or judgmental comment, as in "I feel that you were being a jerk," or assuming negative intentions—for instance, "I feel that you wanted me to fail." Also, as best you can, try to avoid statements about how the other person "made" you feel a certain way, as in "You made me so mad." This doesn't mean that you have to deny your feelings. You can be assertive while also owning your experience, as in "I'm still feeling mad at you for talking about my weight in front of my friends tonight." In healthy relationships, each person has a soft spot for the other, and in hearing words of discouragement, anger, sadness, or frustration (assuming that your feelings are based on reasonable expectations), most likely each of you will want to be responsive to the other's needs.

Communicating Your Needs and Wants

Expressing your needs and wants is also an important element of compassionate assertiveness. Certain statements, like "I really want us to spend more time with the kids," or the counterpart, "I realize that I'm wanting more time for myself," (rather than a focus on "you" and "your faults") can let the other person know you are willing to express yourself for the sake of your relationship. Try to be specific and concrete ("I felt very disappointed when I heard you tease your sister this morning" instead of "You were mean to your sister").

As best you can, in a friendly way let the other person know what it is that you want or need. Include *I-messages* when making requests and expressing your needs, rather than focusing on the faults or mistakes of others. Some examples of I-messages are "I want/need/would like…

…to feel more appreciated than I do right now."

…for us to do more fun things together" (omit "for a change").

...to know that you are okay" (omit "instead of leaving me hanging").

...to relax for a while before dinner" (omit "for once").

Even as you express your feelings and needs, make an effort to pause after each sentence to allow the other person to respond, rather than going on and on, and try not to interrupt. In addition to expressing a feeling, it can often be very helpful to explain *why* you feel that way. For instance, when you say, "I'm *concerned because* since you've been spending so much time on the Internet your grades have dropped from A's and B's to B's and C's," you are stating your feelings, noting a correlation with a behavior you believe is a contributing factor, and being specific and concrete. Many of these techniques are described in *Nonviolent Communication* (Rosenberg 2003), an excellent book on healthy communication.

Making Reasonable Requests

After you have listened carefully to the other person's point of view and asked clarifying questions, if the problem has not been resolved, explain why it matters to you. You could then state what you would like to have happen next or ask for the other person's ideas about how to solve the problem. You may be tempted to express yourself in an angry way, but an aggressive approach could backfire. You might assume that the other person knows what you want, but it could be important for you to be explicit. Or you might be tempted to stomp off, saying, "Just forget it." These extremes are not likely to serve you, or the other person, well.

On the other hand, if your request or expectation is reasonable and your intention is to benefit both of you and your relationship, you will have a good chance of success. Statements and questions like "It would mean a lot to me...," "How would you feel about...?" "What do you think we should do ...?" or "In the future could you...?" will show the other person that you are looking not for control but for mutual cooperation that will benefit both of you. Again, being specific and concrete and explaining why you are making the request will help you be clear and get your point across in a friendly way: "I really need your help with the gardening on the weekends [expressing your needs and making a request] *because* it's too big a job for me and I know that we both want our yard to look nice [the reasons behind the request]."

Expressing Gratitude

As was more thoroughly discussed in chapter 3, gratitude is one of the most important elements in a healthy relationship. When communicating using compassionate assertiveness, remember to express appreciation whenever someone is responsive to your concerns or requests. There are so many times when "Thank you" or "I really appreciate it" can make the difference between someone feeling happy to have worked out a problem with you and feeling resentful.

This is an especially effective technique when you also acknowledge the potential effort or inconvenience that the other person is agreeing to in order to accommodate your needs. Even if you don't get everything you want, your gratitude provides powerful positive reinforcement and a strong incentive for the other person to remain responsive to your needs. Here are a few examples that could apply to a variety of situations:

- "Thank you so much for taking the time to talk with me."

- "I really appreciate that you are willing to work with me to fix the problem."

- "Thanks for hearing me out, even though we remember things differently."

Now let's see how one woman used compassionate assertiveness not only to express her own feelings, needs, and wants, but also to solicit and respond in a caring way to the feelings, needs, and wants of others.

Li's Story

Li had a history of jumping to conclusions and judging others, which led her to feel angry and frustrated. Most times she held her feelings inside, but then she often found herself feeling bitter and resentful. Unfortunately, people often responded to her interpersonal style with defensiveness or avoidance, which further fueled her tendency to blame and criticize others. As she learned compassionate assertiveness, Li learned to defer making assumptions and attributions of blame and to raise concerns when she felt it was important to do so, rather than waiting until anger dominated her thoughts and feelings. The following are a few of the successes in not jumping to conclusions that Li reported during a one-week period:

○ Li invited a friend to a party via e-mail. The day before the party, her friend still hadn't sent an RSVP. In the past, Li might have jumped to the conclusion that her friend was being inconsiderate, and she might have called and angrily asked her friend why she hadn't responded to the e-mail. Instead Li recognized that there may have been a good reason she hadn't heard back, called her friend, and asked in a friendly way, "Did you get the e-mail I sent you a few weeks ago about the party I'm having tomorrow?" To Li's relief, her friend said that she thought for sure that she had responded to the invitation and said that the party was on her calendar.

○ Li's sister (who lived in a time zone two hours behind Li's) woke Li up one night when she called at 11:30. Although Li remembered previous times when her sister had accidentally called her late at night, she stopped herself from saying, "It's awfully late to be calling me. You woke me up." Instead she allowed herself to consider that there might be a legitimate reason for the late-night call. She asked, "Are you all right?" As it happened, her sister was distraught because of some bad news she had gotten that day from her doctor and apologized for calling so late but said she really needed to talk with her. Li was very glad she had waited to hear what the call was about before saying anything about the lateness of the hour and was thus able to give her sister the support and encouragement she needed.

Here's how Li handled a few situations in which she used compassionate assertiveness to express her feelings, state her needs and wants, and make a request:

○ Li's children were tumbling around and shouting at each other. Although she suspected that they were fighting, she held back her judgment. Rather than yelling at them to stop, she walked into the room and said, "Whoa, you guys are making a lot of noise [her observation]. What's going on [a neutral question]?" It turned out that they were roughhousing but not fighting. Li told the children to sit down. She took a deep breath and said, "I know that roughhousing is fun [assuming benign intentions], but I'm afraid you could hit your head on a piece of furniture or that something could get broken [why she is concerned]. Not only that, I get really upset when I hear yelling indoors [expressing her needs]. I need for you to do that kind of playing outside [clear and concrete expectations]."

○ Li's husband, Rob, was late for dinner, didn't call, and didn't answer his cell phone. She was tempted to confront him when he got home by complaining, "I made a nice dinner for us and now it's cold. Why didn't you call?" Instead, when he arrived she said, "Hi. I was wondering where you were [neutral comment]." Rob explained that his boss had asked him to stop by his office just as he was leaving work. Then when he finally got away and was on his way home he thought to call her and let her know he'd be late but realized he had left his cell phone at work. She followed up with "I know that you didn't do it on purpose [assuming benign intentions] but I'm really disappointed because I made a special dinner [expressing her feelings]." He responded, "I'm sorry. I'll really try harder to give you a heads-up if I'm running late." Rob then asked if he could make it up to her by cooking or taking her out for dinner that weekend. They then ate dinner, and she acknowledged that maybe eating reheated food wasn't so bad after all [humble self-disclosure].

When the Criticism Is about You

As hard as it may be to make a request or initiate a discussion about a problem or concern, it can be even more difficult to manage criticism and expressions of dissatisfaction when they are aimed at you. We have all been on the receiving end of a complaint or a request, and when that happens the reptilian fight, flight, or freeze reaction and the corresponding emotion—anger, fear, or shutting down—may be hard to rein in. Sometimes it is hard to admit our weaknesses and flaws, but if you can do so you will benefit from it. Make an effort to remember that everyone makes mistakes and that you can model the change you want to see in others by responding to other people's criticisms of you in a thoughtful way.

Even when you are feeling threatened, try to think of feedback as an opportunity to improve yourself, and even if you did make a mistake, remember that having flaws doesn't make you (or anyone else) less of a person. If you are lucky, the other person will use a caring and friendly approach in giving you feedback. But even if she does not, it's an opportunity for you to give her the benefit of the doubt and assume that her intention is to help you improve yourself. If the person is unskillful in addressing a concern, try not to take it personally. Remember that she may have her own problems or other causes and conditions that make it hard for her to show you the care and concern she would want for herself.

Whatever her approach may be, try to respond in an open and receptive manner. Assuming that her criticism is valid and her request is reasonable, this could include the following:

- Listen and learn: Make sure you understand what the concern is ("So do you wish that I would have…?" "It sounds like you were hoping that…" "It sounds like you are assuming…" or "Are you thinking that I…?").

- Try to assess her feelings and assumptions ("Are you angry with me?" "You look really upset," or "What do you think my intentions were?").

- Acknowledge that the problem may have impacted her ("That must have been annoying/upsetting/confusing for you" or "I wasn't aware that you felt that way."

- Share your own feelings and perspective in a humble way ("Yes, that's something I'm trying to work on/something that is hard for me" or "I'm confused because I thought that…") and share your intentions ("I hadn't intended to offend/hurt/inconvenience you…").

- Swallow your pride and apologize in a heartfelt manner ("I know I blew it and I'm sorry" or "I really feel bad about that and hope you'll accept my apology"). By doing this you not only mobilize the other person's naturally forgiving and nurturing nature, but also are modeling healthy humility.

o Find out what the request is and figure out where to go from there by asking something like "What would you like me to do now/in the future?" or "How can I make it up to you/make things better?"

Playfulness and Humor: Strengthening the Ties That Bind

Any discussion of communication, even when talking about problem situations, is not complete without mentioning humor. As human beings, we are naturally drawn to humor, and it is good for us, too. There is evidence that laughter not only helps elevate our mood but is a healthy activity that increases blood flow, strengthens the immune system, reduces muscle pain, and lowers blood sugar (Martin 2006, 309–34). And when you use playfulness in an affectionate way to manage potential problems, the bonding hormones that are released can benefit your relationship, too (Aune 2002).

Countless arguments and disagreements have been softened, resolved, or even prevented by the judicious application of humor. We all know people who are masters at this. They may have many flaws, but somehow their wit endears them to others despite their limitations. Many of us are not as naturally gifted as these people, but we can all learn to use a light touch to relieve tension and help us remember not to take ourselves—or life—too seriously. My mother demonstrated this playful quality years ago on her birthday, an event that my father wasn't always very attentive about. While packing his lunch before he left for work, she slipped a piece of paper inside my father's sandwich, between the meat and the lettuce. On it she had written, "Roses are red, violets are blue, if you don't have a present for me, don't come home." When he bit into his sandwich at lunchtime he literally got the message (and a good laugh from his buddies, too).

When you are upset with someone, or the other way around, try to look at the big picture and remind yourself that imperfection is the human condition and that trying to convince others that you are always right is a misguided effort. In fact, a lot of healthy humor is based on a good-natured recognition of our own (and each other's) flaws and foibles, so you might as well enjoy the ride and use the gift of laughter to smooth life's rough edges. As many wise older people remind us, if you don't sweat the small stuff and can resist taking things too seriously, you have learned two of the most important secrets to living a full, rich life.

While playful humor and affectionate teasing may not always be appropriate when addressing serious concerns, you can often prevent small issues from turning into big problems by using this approach to get your point across while defusing defensiveness or hostility. Taking unfair criticism one step further can be effective: when someone really overreacts to a small oversight on your part, try saying "That was so terrible. I don't know how you put up with me." Exaggeration can be effective too: when your child doesn't respond when you greet her, what if you said, "If you don't answer me I'll have to call the manners police"? Affectionate teasing can also keep things light: when your friend forgets to make a restaurant reservation, try something like "Luckily it wasn't a plane reservation or I'd have to kill you." Then there's paradox, such as "Whatever you do, don't put gas in the car; I love to live on the edge." And the most valuable is self-deprecating humor. When you make a mistake, for instance, try making a comment like "That's why I'm president of the idiots' club." Whatever you try, the most important consideration is that playfulness should not be used as a form of veiled hostility or with the intention of humiliating the other person.

Communicating Using Compassionate Assertiveness, Step by Step

1. **Initiate the conversation.** Stick to the facts, state an observation or impression, or ask a question.

2. **Engage in a dialogue.** Solicit the other person's perspective and perceptions.

3. **Communicate your feelings.** Express your emotions in a clear but calm and caring way.

4. **Use playful humor when possible.** Avoid veiled hostility, and don't take yourself too seriously.

5. **Express your needs.** Own your wants and needs rather than attacking the other person.

6. **Make a request.** Share ideas to find a reasonable mutual solution.

7. **Express appreciation.** You will increase goodwill if you end the conversation graciously.

Consider the Implications for Your Interpersonal Style

❧ If you have an enthusiastic interpersonal style, you may be good at approaching others in a compassionate way, but you may have to work harder to accept constructive criticism.

❧ If you have a discerning interpersonal style, it may be fairly easy for you to communicate your feelings and needs, but your challenge may be to elicit the perspective of the other person.

❧ If you have an open-minded personality style, you may be good at listening to the other person's perspective, but you may have to focus more on deciding and expressing what it is that you really want or need.

In this chapter you have seen how clear and caring communication can help you share your feelings and needs with others in a friendly way and also help you stay steady when criticism comes your way. Often you will find that problems can be resolved fairly easily when both people agree that the request being made is a reasonable one.

But what about circumstances where the other person fully understands what you are asking of him but resists because he thinks he is right or because he has competing needs or different values? What about times when you feel that the other person's expectations of you are unreasonable or not workable for you? In these kinds of situations your communication skills alone may not be enough to resolve the problem, and you may need to use conflict resolution skills. In the next chapter you will become acquainted with how to use the compassionate assertiveness version of negotiation in resolving conflict, and you will then have the full complement of tools in your compassionate assertiveness toolbox. Let's now turn to a way of negotiating that can lead to a win-win solution, even when an agreement seems out of reach.

CHAPTER 9

Using Negotiation Skills to Resolve Conflicts

Sometimes an interpersonal problem is basically one of communication. And as we saw in the last chapter, the ability of both people to communicate their needs and feelings can successfully resolve many of the concerns that are part of day-to-day life.

But what about when caring and clear communication are not enough to resolve a problem? In this chapter we will look at different dimensions of disagreements and build on all you have learned so far so that you can resolve conflicts peacefully and respectfully. Using compassionate assertiveness will help you transform difficulties into opportunities to enhance your relationships. When you need to solve a human problem, two heads are better than one, and a sincere effort to solve that problem based on what both people agree is reasonable and fair—rather than trying to "win" by attacking or controlling the other person—is the healthiest path to a fulfilling relationship.

Be aware that skillful negotiation can help in just about any difficult interpersonal situation, including with your spouse, child, relative, boss, coworker, friend, or neighbor. This means you can apply compassionate assertiveness in a variety of circumstances.

Disagreements Can Be Good for You

Although you may want to get your own way, if you look back over the years you will probably acknowledge that it would not have benefited you if this were always the case. We do not always use perfect judgment, nor do we have the knowledge or maturity to always know what is best. This goes for other people as well.

Therefore, trust that it is best if neither person in a relationship has too much power. One of my favorite quotes is "All power tends to corrupt and absolute power corrupts absolutely" (Acton 1887). This applies not only to political issues, but also to human relationships. This is why healthy relationships involve shared power and are built on mutual concern and compassion for the other. When problems arise, if you can both communicate your needs and wants, weigh a variety of options, and work out mutually beneficial solutions, you will discover one of the best ways to enhance your relationships.

I know some people who relish arguing and debating with each other. Discussions may be heated, points scored, and both people feel energized by the process. This sparring style can invigorate a relationship, but only if the arguing is noncontentious and is in the context of a mutually respectful relationship. Even raising one's voice to make a point is not always destructive if it is used for emphasis and not to insult or intimidate the other person. In contrast, when arguments feel like or are intended to be personal attacks or involve judging the other person, the relationship—beyond the immediate disagreement at hand—may be in trouble.

Compassionate assertiveness, on the other hand, involves a willingness to use a gentle and caring approach to dealing with potential conflict. Developing the ability to face problems and to see them as ways to strengthen your relationships—rather than as threats—could be one of the most important skills you will ever learn.

An Invitation: You Can't Always Get What You Want

Think about an interpersonal experience when you wanted something to be a certain way, and it just didn't turn out the way you had hoped. Looking back on it now, was this a bad thing in every way? Did anything positive come out of it, or did you learn anything from the experience that helped you become the person you are today?

Now think about a time when you were able to press your agenda or insisted upon getting your way. Was there was a negative consequence? If so, what do you think you could have done differently?

Addressing Problems

As discussed previously, if you have a legitimate concern or a reasonable request, or if you feel that someone is harming you in some way, you have a responsibility to yourself and to the other person to address the problem. You have already laid down a foundation of compasssion, gratitude, and patience. You have worked to tame grasping, fear, anger, judging, and impatience. You have sought to see the whole truth of the situation with clear eyes, have paid attention to your own feelings and needs and those of the other person, and have made an effort to communicate in a clear and caring way. If the problem has still not been resolved, you can begin a negotiation process using these now-familiar compassionate assertiveness principles to guide you:

○ Actions are the result of complex causes and consequences.

○ Actions have consequences.

○ Intentions matter.

○ Follow the middle way.

The ability to negotiate effectively is not important only in your personal relationships. It is also valuable in the hierarchical and sometimes competitive workplace, where you are evaluated by supervisors, collaborate with colleagues, and may need to evaluate the work of subordinates. In these cases, too, careful attention to people's intentions, the causes and conditions contributing to their behavior, and the potential consequences of both your actions and theirs will help steer you through the process.

The Process of Negotiating

The negotiation process in compassionate assertiveness combines principles of Buddhist philosophy and cognitive behavioral psychology with the literature on negotiations, primarily used in the worlds of diplomacy and business. *Getting to Yes* (Fisher, Ury, and Patton 1991) bears mentioning: many of its points about negotiating fair and reasonable agreements in the business world are quite consistent with the compassionate assertiveness approach to cultivating healthy personal relationships. These include (1) recognizing that different people have different needs and perceptions, (2) focusing on solving the problem, rather than just trying to get your own way by attacking the other person, (3) being open to a variety of possible solutions, and (4) seeking a reasonable solution.

I'm Right and You're Wrong

When clear communication reveals a conflict of opinions, needs, or values, both individuals might believe that they are right and the other person is wrong. In these cases, negotiation skills can come to the rescue. Here is an example of this kind of conflict and how two individuals came to a reasonable solution.

○ *Chris and Gary's Story*

Chris and Gary were roommates. While they got along in most ways, Chris was frustrated because while he always cleaned up after himself in the kitchen, Gary often left his dirty dishes in the sink. Chris thought that Gary was a slob. Not only was Chris disgusted by the mess in the sink, he worried about it attracting bugs, or worse. Gary thought that Chris was being a neat freak who needed to back off and let him wash the dishes once the sink filled up with dirty dishes. Each thought the other was being unreasonable.

Chris and Gary were both familiar with compassionate assertiveness techniques. They were able to appreciate that the other person was really a good guy and an excellent roommate in almost every way, which set up an atmosphere conducive for working the problem out. The problematic dynamic between them regarding this issue was one that is familiar to most of us: one person was upset about the comparatively low standards of the other, who in turn felt that he was being unfairly attacked. Let's see how they worked it out.

Chris: "This sink is full of your dirty dishes. I've asked you before to clean up after yourself, and now I'm starting to get pissed off. I cleaned up after you twice this week because I'm worried that we'll start seeing roaches in this place. You're a great roommate in almost every other way, but this is really not okay."

Gary: "I didn't ask you to wash them; besides, I can't see why this is such a big deal. And I've told you that I'll eventually get around to it, and would be happy to wash your dishes while I'm at it. And sometimes I feel like not doing the dishes just because of your nagging. If I wanted to be nagged, I'd get married."

Chris: "Very funny. Look, I don't like to bug you, but I just can't stand the mess. Let's figure something out."

Gary: "I'm up for it. Got any ideas?"

Chris: "What about alternating days? Then you would only have to wash the dishes three or four times a week, I wouldn't nag you, and the sink would be clean."

Gary: "Sounds good in theory, but knowing me, I'd let my day go and you'd be even madder. What if we just used paper plates and cups, and plastic utensils?"

Chris: "It would be good for avoiding dirty dishes in the sink, but I don't like adding to landfills, plus I don't like eating off paper plates, and I can think of better ways to spend my money."

Gary: "Hmmm. Well, what if I bought disposables and didn't use your dishes?"

Chris: "That might work. Hey, since we each have our own set of dishes, another possibility would be to get a big airtight plastic container, and you could use your own dishes and keep them in there until you're ready to wash them, or you could use disposables. If you decide not to destroy our planet by using paper and plastic, you can use my pots and pans and I'll wash them."

Gary: "I think we've got a plan. Let's try it out and see how it goes."

In this case, the roommates were able to stay focused on the problem and refrained from attacking each other as people. They both showed a willingness to do a bit more for the other person if he would compromise a little. Gary and Chris were also willing to take responsibility for their own feelings and attitudes. They floated some ideas by each other that might meet both of their needs and finally came up with a solution they could both live with. Finally, they agreed to try out a plan and see how it would work. While neither got 100 percent of what he wanted, they were both satisfied with the outcome, and each felt that the other tried to accommodate his needs.

When the Other Person Reacts Negatively

A lot of people are afraid to raise concerns with someone because when they do so the other person explodes with anger, retaliates with a countercriticism, or stomps off in frigid silence. If this has ever happened to you, you may have found yourself walking on eggshells for fear of setting off an incident that could make things worse instead of better.

In these cases remember to be mindful of the causes and conditions that have led to that kind of behavior. Maybe the other person observed destructive arguing when he was growing up or has been on the receiving end of rage or avoidance reactions when he has tried to address a problem with others. Or maybe he has learned that he can fend off requests or criticisms by yelling at, tuning out, or avoiding the other person.

If the other person reacts negatively when you raise a concern, you may need to ask yourself some hard, honest questions to see if you have unintentionally contributed to the problem in some way. Do you criticize him often but not pay attention to the things you appreciate about him? Do you use words that are inflammatory, nag him, or make unreasonable requests? Do you always back down when he blows up or blows you off, thereby inadvertently encouraging his aggression? In these difficult situations it is often helpful to set up a time to talk together at the other person's convenience, letting him know you've noticed some tension between you that you would like to address for the sake of your relationship. When you do sit down together, try to use the communication and negotiation techniques in this chapter and the previous one to guide you.

By cultivating gratitude and patience, and looking at your own frustration, fear, or anger, you can work on exploring your feelings and behavior in an honest way. Try to acknowledge to yourself and to the other person any missteps of your own that may have contributed to the problem. This does not mean ignoring serious concerns, but rather acknowledging the contributing factors, doing what you can to change your own behavior when appropriate, and negotiating in good faith with your eye on improving the situation rather than winning for the sake of proving your point or exerting control.

Sometimes Actions Speak Louder Than Words

While many negotiations are primarily verbal exchanges, creative problem solving using compassionate assertiveness can also include taking action. Here's an example:

○ *Dave and Nancy's Story*

Dave came to me for help improving his communication and assertiveness skills. He was a very tidy man who always cleaned up after himself and often picked up after his wife, Nancy, who was on the messy side. Dave was especially annoyed that Nancy had a habit of leaving her shoes in the middle of the floor. After picking up after her on several occasions, he finally brought the problem to her attention. She agreed with him, apologized, and then quickly picked up several pairs of shoes that she had left lying around. However, her improvement was short-lived, and before long, in spite of additional requests, she fell back into her old habits. Dave found himself getting more and more angry and frustrated, and he knew that his reminders just weren't working. He wanted to create a change, but without yelling or nagging.

Using his compassionate assertiveness skills, Dave spent some time thinking about Nancy's many positive qualities. He asked himself how he would want Nancy to handle the situation if she were upset with him and realized that he would want her to do some problem-solving with him rather than blow up. He decided to talk with Nancy about it. He told her that he had tried picking up after her and nagging, but neither worked, and he was starting to get very annoyed. He asked if she was willing to have a consequence, and she agreed that it might be needed. They decided that whenever she left her shoes in the middle of the floor, he would put them on top of the bed, on her side.

They tried this and it did the trick. She worked hard to remember to keep her shoes out of the middle of the room and quickly got into the habit of doing so. After that, Dave usually ignored the occasional pair of shoes left lying around, and Nancy began to automatically put them away when she saw them. The problem was solved without aggression or resentment on either side, and both Dave and Nancy were happy with the results.

Handling Criticism and Unreasonable Demands

Have you ever felt blindsided by what felt to you like an unreasonable request or by criticism, especially delivered in a humiliating or aggressive manner? When this happens to you, you'll want to be able to respond calmly. You can do so if you make an effort to be patient and to assume benign—or at least neutral—intentions, and remember that if you allow someone to intimidate you or to persuade you to do something against your better judgment it won't be good for either of you.

Sometimes you will have an immediate skillful response; sometimes you won't. The important thing is to rein in your neuroendocrine system's emergency responders, because if you are feeling an impulse to protect yourself at all costs you may say or do something you'll regret. If you are being criticized, it's better to give yourself some time to look at the whole picture, including your thoughts and emotions, and to consider that the person's criticisms might be gifts that can guide you to be the best you can be. You might remember the old saying that our critics can teach us more than our friends. I believe this is true: even an unjustified or hurtful criticism can be a valuable lesson. When responding to what you feel is an unreasonable request, bear in mind that the other person may not be aware that he is overstepping boundaries, and also be aware of the causes and conditions that might have led him to have that expectation of you. Don't forget to look inward as well. Is it possible that you are being stingy, withholding, or selfish? If so, work with that awareness and see if you can experience the challenge of being pushed beyond your comfort zone as an opportunity for personal growth.

Here are some phrases to keep in mind when you believe you are being unfairly criticized or being leaned on to do something you don't feel is right for you. Remember that it is better to delay giving a response than to give in, get mad, run away, or shut down:

- "It sounds like you're really upset with me."

- "I don't understand. Where does this come from?"

- "I'm not comfortable with your question/request."

- "I'm having a hard time taking in what you're saying because of the way that you're saying it."

- "I don't believe that you have the whole picture."

- "I'm sorry you feel that way. What do you think I/we should do?"

- "I'm really caught off guard. Can we talk about it tomorrow?"

○ "This is so unexpected—I'll need some time to think about it before I respond."

○ "I appreciate your concern, but I see things differently."

○ "Maybe you'd like me to feel differently, but I don't."

○ "Maybe you wish that…"

○ "This isn't (or "that wouldn't be") workable for me."

○ "Your reaction/question/request/criticism doesn't feel reasonable to me."

If Negotiation Doesn't Work

Even though we can't always get what we want, isn't it reasonable to at least sometimes get our way? Have you ever been in a relationship where the other person always insists on doing things her way? There are some relationships where one person makes all the decisions and the other person is fine with this; but in this day and age, most healthy relationships involve give and take. If the other person never budges, or reacts very negatively when you challenge her decisions, offer constructive criticism, or make a reasonable request, or if your efforts to negotiate change or seek outside help are not effective, it may be necessary to walk away from the relationship. In fact, from a compassionate assertiveness position, it is better for both of you if you end a relationship rather than let someone continue to behave in ways that bring out the worst in you or that harm you.

Be prepared: if you do need to end a relationship, you may have to face a number of emotional, social, financial, or even legal stresses. Divorces, family feuds, and legal battles over child custody or inheritances lead to rage and revenge for many, but try to cultivate a different mind-set. Even if you need to end the relationship, see if you can keep a soft spot in your heart for that other person and even forgive her for the pain she has caused you. After all, you both have strengths and flaws, joys and sorrows, hopes and dreams. And at one time there was something good there for both of you. You can move on and do what you need to do to take care of yourself, but even if it's just for your own sake, try to allow yourself to let go of resentments and hatred and, ultimately, to honor the common humanity that you share.

Difficult endings can also occur in new relationships. If you see early signs that your reasonable requests or needs do not seem very important to the other person, you need to ask yourself if this is a pattern you are willing to accept. Sometimes in a new dating relationship one person wants more time, attention, or involvement than the other does. This is not usually a question of good or bad or right or wrong, but rather a difference in pacing, expectations, or values. Although ending a new relationship is different from ending an established one, what both have in common is that there may come a time when it is best for both of you to move on so you can each meet someone with whom you are more compatible.

Ending a relationship may be your decision, the other person's decision, or a mutual decision. If the ending of a relationship is not your choice, it is an opportunity to think about whether there are changes that you need to make for the sake of your future relationships. If you are ending the relationship, it is an opportunity to do so in as kind a way as possible. In either case, be compassionate toward yourself and the other person during this process. Try to rise above hatred or wishes for revenge. After all, if the other person didn't have any redeeming qualities, or if you didn't share good times, you would not have been in the relationship in the first place. At the same time, give yourself permission to free yourself from a situation that wasn't a good one for you.

○ *Laurie's Story: A Tale with Two Endings*

Laurie had learned about compassionate assertiveness and was using it to help her resist pressure from people (especially men) who wanted her to do things she didn't feel comfortable with. She had recently met Sam through an online dating service. She liked him but wasn't sure how much, and wanted to get to know him better. On their third date, after they had both had a few drinks at a bar, Sam invited her to his apartment. She sensed the possibility of his wanting to move to a sexual relationship, which she did not want to do at that stage in their relationship. In the past Laurie would have felt that she couldn't say no unless she was sure there would be a problem, and she might well have given in despite misgivings. This time she was willing to pay attention to her feelings of caution and to trust her gut reaction that she didn't want to put herself in a potentially awkward situation. Since they both had been drinking, she was also worried that her own compromised judgment, or his, might lead to a sexual encounter. Laurie told Sam that although she liked him she really didn't feel ready to go to his place. He denied any intention of making a move on her and then said that it seemed she did not trust him. Laurie replied, "It's true that I probably don't trust you as much as I would if I knew you better. But trust is not the main issue. The main issue is that you are trying to talk me into doing something I don't feel comfortable doing. I like you. You may have innocent intentions, but I've already told you no, and I don't like feeling pushed."

Sam then explained that there was a sports game he wanted to watch. Although she wasn't really into sports bars, Laurie then suggested going to one to watch the game there. At that point Sam said he preferred to watch the game at his place and that maybe they should just end their date. Despite some temptation to give in so he would not leave feeling hurt or angry, Laurie replied calmly that maybe that was a good idea and added that she hoped he'd enjoy the game. They gave each other an awkward hug and left. Laurie decided not to initiate the next contact, but to wait and see what happened next. She told herself that if he didn't call, she would know he wasn't the right person for her.

Here are two potential endings to this story. They are both happy endings:

First scenario. The following week, Sam did call, and they went out again. This time he did not pressure her to go to his place. Apparently, he had given some thought to her comments. He said he would wait for her to invite him to her place or offer to go to his place, and he apologized for having put pressure on her. She expressed appreciation for his comments and found herself thinking more fondly of him. They continued to date and enjoyed a healthy and mutually respectful relationship that progressed at a pace with which they both felt comfortable. This experience helped Laurie recognize that Sam cared for her and accepted her values.

Second scenario. Sam never called Laurie again. Although she was a bit disappointed, she figured that, unlike her, he was probably into casual sex, so her resistance to his pressure was a deal breaker for him. She felt relieved, and even a little proud of herself that she could use her newly acquired compassionate assertiveness skills to help her with an old problem. Most important, she could feel at peace, knowing that she was able to hold to her values instead of being controlled by her fear of being rejected or hurting Sam's feelings. Six months later she met someone who was on the same wavelength, and their relationship proceeded at a pace that felt right to both of them.

Negotiating Using Compassionate Assertiveness, Step by Step

1. Lay your foundation of gratitude and patience on a day-to-day basis.

2. Draw upon your communication skills throughout the process.

3. Seek to understand the other person's point of view.

4. Recognize that your goal is to solve the problem, not attack the person.

5. Express your own feelings and needs in a calm manner.

6. Include the other person's needs in your mind as you negotiate ways to solve the problem.

7. Don't try to force a solution. Allow yourself and the other person time to mull things over if needed.

8. If you don't get what you want, try to take it in stride. Focus on the big picture, including positives, and try to cultivate patience for yourself and the other person.

9. If over time negotiation after negotiation fails, consider making a change in your life.

Consider the Implications for Your Interpersonal Style

- If you have an enthusiastic interpersonal style, you will generally be skilled at approaching a problem in a friendly way, but when you are negotiating be careful not to let your ego push you to prove your point and try to control the other person.

- If you have a discerning interpersonal style, you will most likely be able to set limits with others, but beware of letting anger cloud your ability to do so in a kind manner.

- If you have an open-minded interpersonal style, your sense of fairness will serve you well. However, because you may get confused about what to do, you need to be careful not to agree to do something that you really don't want to do and then "forget" to do it.

In this chapter you have seen how you can use the compassionate assertiveness skills discussed earlier to negotiate a solution to a problem. In the final part of this book you will see how compassionate assertiveness works—step by step—in the various domains of your life: with your partner, with your family, and with the outside world.

PART 4

Applying Compassionate Assertiveness in Love and in Life

CHAPTER 10

Compassionate Assertiveness for Couples

Tanya had been frustrated for months about her husband, Ani. As smart, kind, fun, and generous as he generally was, after work he was almost always distant and withdrawn. And almost every day, even on the weekends, it seemed like all he wanted to do in the evening was watch TV. He even wanted to eat dinner in front of the TV set every night, which left Tanya feeling ignored and increasingly annoyed.

Tanya decided that maybe she wasn't doing enough to make dinners together romantic and appealing. Tonight she would surprise him. She'd make his favorite foods, set a lovely table, and have a nice conversation about their day, just like they used to do when they were first dating. She cooked a lovely meal, set the table, put on some romantic music, and waited for Ani to come home.

When Ani came through the front door, Tanya went over to greet him. She hung up his coat and gave him a kiss. He kissed her back and hugged her for a few seconds, and then went to take a shower and get into his sweatpants and T-shirt. When he came downstairs, Tanya excitedly showed him the table with the lovely dinner she had prepared.

"Oh, that's really nice, Tanya," Ani said, "but I'm really tired and stressed from another hard day at work, and I don't want to make an event out of dinner tonight. How about if we just eat in front of the TV?"

Tanya didn't want to give up so easily. "But we almost never eat dinner at the table, and after all I did to make this nice dinner, the least you could do is push yourself a little and give me some of your attention and time."

"Look," he replied, "tonight is Monday night football, and the last thing I want to do is talk to you when there's something else I am really interested in doing. If you had checked with me before you did all this I could have saved you the time and trouble."

By this point Tanya was on the verge of tears. "You're so unavailable! If you really cared about my feelings you'd be more grateful and spend just twenty minutes of your precious time giving me some attention."

They went back and forth this way for about ten minutes. Finally, Ani blew up. "You're just trying to control me and make me someone I'm not. If you're that unhappy with me tonight, I'll just go to a sports bar and grab a hamburger and a beer there. At least there no one will be hassling me." And with that he grabbed his jacket and stormed out of the house.

What went wrong? Whose fault was it? And was there any way this disastrous outcome to what started out with good intentions could have been prevented? These kinds of situations, which can leave both members of a couple frustrated and angry, are not that uncommon. In this chapter we'll look at romantic relationships and learn about some of the differences between two people in a couple, differences that—depending on how they are handled—can either lead to problems or enhance their relationship.

The Perils and Promise of Romantic Relationships

Whether you are in the first blush of love, have been with your loved one for decades, or are anywhere in between, a romantic relationship can offer an experience unlike any other. New love blazes with the intensity of a freshly stoked fire, infusing us with excitement and the anticipation of endless possibilities, with both parties seeing each other through rose-colored glasses and being on their best behavior. Long-standing love can create a warm glow deep within us that can sustain us through the ups and downs of life, but what used to be cute can now be annoying, and the two parties can start taking each other for granted. At all stages, these are relationships of vulnerability and interdependence, relationships that call for an open heart and the willingness of two imperfect persons to share their lives with each other.

When problems come up with your partner—and they will—you will need courage and gentle strength, as well as a variety of communication and negotiation skills, to successfully address sensitive issues, including trust, independence, and control.

At our best, we search for ways to soften the barriers between us, try to refrain from judging ourselves or each other, and try to grow and change with our partner; and we work on being patient and tolerant with the differences we may not be able to change in ourselves and each other. At our worst, we may try to control our partner: to bend him to our will, keep him at a safe distance, or criticize him to make him perfect. Or we may deny our own needs in order to keep from losing him.

Successfully navigating these tricky waters involves looking at the differences between you and your partner with clear eyes. As individual human beings with different backgrounds and upbringings, you may have to adjust to differing styles, expectations, needs, and values.

Some of those differences may be related to gender. Gender-based behavioral differences may be just one aspect of any relationship, but they are an important one (Kimura 1999). As we look at differences between the sexes, please note that male and female tendencies can be thought of as overlapping bell curves, so "female" tendencies may occur more strongly in some men than in some women, and vice versa. Even same-sex couples have different degrees of what are often considered male and female characteristics. Therefore, many of the same problems that come up for heterosexual couples can also be seen in gay or lesbian couples. Furthermore, the nature–nurture debate should be kept in mind as you read this chapter, because no one knows exactly which of our traits are inborn and which are learned.

Male–Female Differences

When it comes to intimate relationships, men and women are much more alike than they are different. After all, don't we all want to feel that we are attractive, desirable, and competent in the eyes of our beloved? Still, the differing reproductive and parenting functions between the sexes have led to certain biological differences between them (Pinker 2002). Our neuroendocrine system—especially testosterone and other "male" chemicals in males and estrogen, oxytocin, and other "female" chemicals in females—plays a major role in these differences. Neuroendocrine messages influence what we look like, how we think, and how we interact with the world. While these differences can lead to misunderstandings and confusion, making an effort to understand and appreciate them as gender related can help you manage the challenges they present, and even celebrate the ways they can enrich your life.

Physical differences. A man's body is designed to compete for sexual partners, protect women and children, hunt for food, and create safe boundaries for his family and social group. These responsibilities require cooperation, but also strength, speed, and the ability to be aggressive when necessary. The physical stature and muscular development of males are geared toward fulfilling these roles. A woman's body, on the other hand, is designed to attract males, bear children, and provide her offspring with nourishment and a safe physical and social environment. These are no small tasks, because human babies are dependent on their parents much longer than the young of any other species.

Cognitive differences. Hormones create small anatomical differences in the brains of males and females that can produce different cognitive styles (Brizendine 2006, 14–15). Strengths in the female cognitive style include empathy (attunement to emotions in others), verbal abilities, and a mindset that promotes bonding. Males, on the other hand, excel at spatial relationships and "systemizing," including analytic and information-based thinking, and are more interested in details, patterns, rules, and logic (Baron-Cohen 2003). (Note: If you would like to take some tests to see where you fall on the continuum between empathy and systemizing, check out Baron-Cohen's book or the website listed in the Resources section.)

Despite certain gender-based tendencies, however, the good news is that your brain has a high degree of *neuroplasticity*, as mentioned in chapter 1. This means that brain function, neural connections, and even anatomical features can change and grow through learning, experience, and practice, thus allowing us to strengthen areas of functioning that may be weak. In other words, you really can teach an old dog new tricks. For instance, boys and men can be successfully encouraged to strengthen their emotional intelligence and language abilities, while girls and women can become stronger in less verbal realms, such as math and science. And it has been shown that males can learn to increase their focus on the process and social context of a conversation, rather than focusing solely on information or outcome, while females can improve their attention to details and facts (Eliot 2009). A client of mine who had frequent disagreements with his wife reported that their relationship improved when he stopped debating facts with her in a competitive way and instead acknowledged that they could have differing but valid perspectives on an issue.

Communication styles. Neuroendocrine differences between the sexes influence how we interact and communicate. Women tend to use language to connect and reach consensus with others, paying close attention to the meaning and the social and emotional context of language. They often use somewhat subjective phrases, such as "I feel" or "I think." In addition, they typically orient their bodies toward each other and use eye contact to assess and respond to each other's facial expressions and other nonverbal cues.

Men, in contrast, generally tend to use language to exchange factual information. In comparison with women, they generally take words and statements more literally and are more interested in results than process. Thus, when a woman is telling a story or describing a problem, the man is likely to ask, "So, what's the bottom line?" or immediately start offering solutions. In addition, men usually orient their bodies somewhat away from each other and avoid long periods of eye contact unless they are trying to establish dominance (Tannen 1990).

Social behavior. Neuroendocrine based differences between men and women affect social behavior as well. For instance, most men tend to be more comfortable than most women in competitive activities, such as sports, and in the types of hierarchical relationships found in work settings with clear leadership and subordinate roles (the military is a good example of this type of organization). They also tend to value self-reliance and independence.

Women, on the other hand, generally enjoy dyadic or small-group bonding experiences that are rich in verbal exchanges and cooperative activities—experiences that are conducive to a female group's shared child-raising responsibilities. Hierarchies and competition are evident in female relationships, but they are generally more subtle and indirect than those of males and are more often focused on social status and physical appearance

(Eliot 2009). Furthermore, there is evidence that in women the fight-or-flight stress reaction is tempered by a "tend and befriend" predisposition to cultivate strong relationships and to engage in a group-based, "circle the wagons" response when a member of their group is threatened. This would have originated as an adaptive survival behavior because women are limited in their ability to fight or flee when caring for dependent offspring (Taylor 2000).

Bridging the Gap

Although biological differences between men and women exist and have certain physical, cognitive, and behavioral effects, there is growing evidence that the influence of these biological differences is not as powerful as was once thought. "Male" hormones, such as testosterone and other androgens, which fuel aggression and competition, are found in small amounts in women, while small amounts of "female" hormones, such as estrogen and oxytocin, are found in males. And interestingly, studies have shown that levels of certain hormones in men change when they become fathers: levels of oxytocin (one of the most important bonding hormones) increase, while testosterone levels decline (Eliot 2009, 269).

It should be noted, however, that while cognitive and emotional differences do exist between males and females at birth, as children grow into adulthood even minor differences in brain anatomy and neurological pathways can be magnified by years of adhering to traditional gender roles, interests, and interactive and cognitive styles, making it more difficult to develop our full potential (Eliot 2009).

What does all this information have to do with improving your relationship with your partner? First, you can recognize and enjoy the overlap in areas of interest, styles, and values between yourself and your partner. Second, you can cultivate gratitude for your gender differences and see them as complementary skills and strengths that can contribute to your happiness as a couple, rather than as a source of conflict. Third, awareness of sex differences can help you avoid unrealistic and unfair expectations about how people of the opposite sex "should" think, feel, and behave. If you can acknowledge that "different" doesn't mean "better" or "worse," this will help you anticipate and resolve potential problems before they undermine your relationship. Let's look at how certain sex differences can manifest themselves in your interactions with your partner, and consider some ways that, with mutual understanding and concern for each other, you can accommodate each other's needs.

Together and apart. One important difference between what most men and women want in a relationship has to do with personal boundaries. Men typically tend more toward boundary-setting and novelty-seeking activities, behaviors that were adaptive when tribes competed for hunting grounds and establishment of settlements. This can translate into men wanting physical activity, their own "space," and adventure. A man may want to spend time on his own or with his male friends engaging in physically demanding projects, shooting hoops, or just having a beer. This is consistent with his hunter-warrior biological legacy, but women often misinterpret the behavior as "avoidant" or "distracting."

Most women, on the other hand, are more geared toward connecting with others, a trait that supports stable environments for raising children. They might want to spend time getting closer to their husband or boyfriend by doing activities as a couple or just talking and getting closer to each other emotionally. This is understandable given females' biologically based emphasis on bonding, but those expectations have the potential to create tension and confusion between them and their male partners, who might feel that they are being "fenced in." (Pinker 2002).

These differing priorities are not insurmountable, however. If you are a man, you can try to recognize that it is unlikely your female partner's efforts to connect with you are intended to control and corral you, and if you are willing to initiate some "together" time, your partner will appreciate it. This time can involve relaxing at home reading the newspaper together, going out to eat, or taking a walk. Or you can do something that involves being physically active together, such as playing tennis or going camping, where you can talk along the way. Using this time to ask her about her day and making an effort to share a bit about what is going on with you will very likely meet her needs, which will then help her be more generous and relaxed when you need some time for yourself.

If you are a woman, you can try allowing silence to settle after you've spoken a sentence or two to your male partner. It's very possible that he'll come forward eventually and fill some of the silence. It may not be as much as you'd like, but it is probably better than the frustration that you might feel when you keep talking and talking in a futile effort to draw him out.

And keep in mind that activities like taking a walk together might get conversations going without his having to look at you head-on. Maybe you can save those long talks at the coffeehouse for get-togethers with your female friends, who will be more likely to appreciate the experience.

How do I love thee? Another important aspect of a relationship is how each partner expresses love and how the other one interprets that effort. Ironically, you can miss your partner's expressions of love if you don't recognize them as such, which can happen when they are different from your own. The book *The Five Love Languages: How to Express Heartfelt Commitment to Your Mate* (Chapman 1995) describes several styles of expressing love, which can at times differ along gender lines. These are (1) verbal affirmation, such as expressions of love, praise, or gratitude; (2) quality time, when there is focused attention on you and your relationship, or you are doing something fun or interesting together; (3) giving gifts, which could include small tokens such as flowers or cards, or big-ticket items like jewelry; (4) acts of service, which are practical things you do to make your partner's life easier, such as doing the laundry, paying the bills, or cooking a nice meal; and (5) physical touch, including holding hands, giving and receiving back rubs, and sexual relations.

Once you are aware of your own ways of expressing love, you can expand your awareness to recognize that there are many ways to show love and caring, and that your way isn't the only way. This can help you recognize and appreciate your partner's acts of love. It also encourages you to consider broadening your view of how love "should" be expressed. If you apply compassionate assertiveness to the concept that there are many ways to express love, your concern for the well-being of your partner can inspire you to find ways to make her happy.

Using compassionate assertiveness with your loved one includes cultivating gratitude and patience, identifying and working with fear and anger, and using mindfulness and skillful communication to increase your awareness of your own feelings, beliefs, and intentions, as well as those of your partner. Feelings of loving-kindness can then bubble up and help you feel that your partner's needs are as important as your own. This does not mean abandoning your preferred ways of showing love, but rather accepting that they may differ from those of your loved one.

You need to let your partner know how you would most enjoy receiving expressions of love from her. But try to recognize that her preferred styles are as valid as yours, even if they are not your favorites. I hope your partner will make an effort to meet your needs, just as I hope that you will try to meet hers. However, if she cannot do so, or if her efforts are not sustained, try to accept her limitations, just as you hope she would accept yours.

What about sex? There is an old saying that men give love in order to get sex, while women give sex in order to get love. While that is not fully accurate, it is true that there are some biologically driven differences that can cause misunderstandings, frustration, and disappointment on both sides. Fortunately, if you are motivated to increase each other's pleasure and satisfaction for the sake of your relationship, many problems can be resolved.

For instance, men, who are biologically programmed to "spread their seed," do not necessarily always merge loving feelings with sexual arousal, and they may be more focused on orgasm than foreplay. In addition, they may value excitement and novelty in their sexual activities. On the other hand, women, who are biologically programmed to ensure that they and their offspring are protected, generally tend to view sex as an intimate experience that implies concern for their welfare and an emotional connection. They generally value words of affection and enjoy nongenital touching before and during foreplay, and they may not be as interested in adventurous sex as their partner. These differences can generally be accommodated if you and your partner can communicate your preferences and needs while being sensitive to your loved one's desires and respectful of each other's limits. Within those parameters, trying different kinds of sex play, if you both agree, can deepen your intimacy while also keeping your sex life spicy.

My advice to men: Before initiating sex, try engaging in a nonromantic fun activity with your partner. Make an effort to include some romantic or warmhearted conversation, as well as affectionate physical touch, which will most likely enhance her enthusiasm and receptivity. During foreplay, take your time and ask what kind of touching would feel good to her, and then try it. If you want to add more spice to your sex life, see what she thinks about trying some playful aggression, such as arm wrestling or a pillow fight.

My advice to women is to communicate what feels good, let him know what to modify, ask him what he would like, and cultivate enthusiasm. After all, he has his own ideas of what is sexually gratifying; at the same time, he finds you desirable and will most likely want to give you pleasure but may not always know quite how to do so. Both men and women need to remember that although willingness to try new things can enhance a relationship, if your partner wants you to do something that is really unpleasant or repugnant to you, it is important to speak up and not give in to pressure but instead look for other ways to give and receive pleasure. Ultimately, if you both want to please each other sexually, it is very likely that your relationship will be enhanced, both in the bedroom and outside of it.

An Invitation: Honor Your Partner's Efforts and Needs

Think about the different ways that people express love and care: (1) words of affirmation, (2) spending quality time together, (3) giving and receiving gifts, (4) acts of service, and (5) physical affection. Rank them in order of importance to you, and see if your partner is willing to do so as well. Share your lists and see if you both are willing to bend for each other.

Reconciling Areas of Conflict, Step by Step

Your relationship with your romantic partner is unique. It is intense and emotionally powerful, and it may be extremely rewarding in many ways. But this also means that when conflicts come up they may be highly charged and can create pain and frustration on both sides.

Fortunately, a compassionate assertiveness approach can help you see these problems as opportunities to deepen your relationship. Think about letting go of your ego for the benefit of your relationship. Consider the benefits of making a commitment to communicate and negotiate more effectively. If the quality of your relationship is important to you, it is worth taking the time and effort to do so.

Now let's go back to our earlier discussion about Tanya and Ani. When they came to me for help it became clear that much of the mutual frustration and unhappiness they felt was related to male-female differences and not personal flaws. I talked with them about how women often want more togetherness through conversation and affection than men do, and men often need more time and space to themselves. They listened carefully and over the next few months they used some of the principles of compassionate assertiveness to work on their problems. Here's how our work helped them deal with their dinnertime dilemma:

○ **Cultivate gratitude.** Each of them set aside a few minutes several times a week to write down, contemplate, or meditate on the positive qualities of the other. This helped them bring to mind the things they appreciated about each other, as well as ways in which they had positively affected each other's lives.

○ **Be mindful of your feelings and beliefs.** When they got upset with each other, I encouraged them to investigate their emotions, thoughts, and beliefs with gentle honesty and without judging them. I asked them to assess whether their assumptions about the other person were really accurate and to check in with each other to see if they were on target. We discussed their criticisms of each other, and they began to see that most of their differences were just differences, not flaws. Each of them tried to see things from the other person's point of view, and they began to ask themselves if their own expectations were reasonable.

○ **Remember that actions are the result of complex causes and conditions.** Tanya wondered if maybe she had contributed to the problem by talking too much or asking Ani too many questions. He began to challenge his assumption that she was just trying to control him, and he asked himself if he would be willing to compromise for the sake of their relationship.

○ **Begin a dialogue.** They sat down and talked when they had privacy and time. Tanya began with this observation: "It seems to me that we've been eating dinner in front of the TV almost every night for months." She listened to his response, including his feelings about it. Here are some responses that many men have:

- o "I disagree. Don't you remember that just last week we ate dinner on the patio?"

- o "I need time to unwind and relax after work and not have to talk."

- o "Since our dinners are usually pizza or fast food, I don't think it's worth the effort to treat them like real meals."

- o "I hate eating dinner at the table. It brings back memories of terrible fights that my parents had at dinnertime when I was growing up."

Tanya tried to hear Ani's response with an open heart and realized that while she thought eating dinner at the table should be a romantic and intimate time together, it did not have the same meaning for him.

- o **Share your feelings while showing empathy.** Tanya acknowledged respect for Ani's feelings and then communicated her feelings and needs. "It sounds like eating dinner at the table doesn't mean the same thing to you that it does to me. For me it's a romantic way to reconnect at the end of the day, so I'd love it if we sat down together; but for you it seems to interfere with your time to unwind." He agreed but acknowledged that it seemed important to her, so he might be willing to compromise.

- o **Seek to negotiate in a caring way.** Here are some of their ideas:

  - o Eat dinner at the table on the weekends. Tanya would make a special dinner for those occasions.

  - o Tanya offered to do more of something that was important to Ani (like doing more yard work) to show her appreciation for his willingness to compromise about dinner.

○ Ani requested alone time. Tanya tried to meet his needs "If you indulge me by eating in the kitchen on the weekends, I won't interrupt you when you are watching sports games."

○ They got playful, and Tanya said, "I'll feed you peeled grapes and wear a negligee!" "Fine," Ani replied. "Just don't turn it into a conversation!"

Together, they came up with an agreement that worked for them. If she had come up with all the ideas and he had vetoed all of them, Tanya could have asked Ani if he had any ideas of his own. This last option is an important one to consider. (Remember that applies to you, too. Just because you raise a concern, this doesn't mean you have to come up with all the possible solutions.)

○ **Forgive limitations.** If Ani wouldn't budge, Tanya might have to decide how important this problem was in the grand scheme of things. She might have to accept this as one of his limitations and remind herself that she had a few as well. She might also recognize that it was not realistic to expect him to meet all her needs. If she enjoyed conversation over a meal with others, maybe she and a friend could arrange to go out to eat or to each other's house for dinner on a regular basis.

○ **Remember that actions have consequences, and intentions matter.** Tanya knew that it would benefit her to think of Ani's needs as well as her own. She wanted to foster intimacy, and had she insisted on just having things her way it would have worked against her intentions. She trusted that there were many ways to promote closeness. Meanwhile, she decided that eating dinner with a girlfriend once a week or so, especially when there was a game on TV, would be a good way to help her relationship with Ani by taking the pressure off him.

> ## *Consider the Implications for Your Interpersonal Style*
>
> ❧ If you have an enthusiastic interpersonal style, you will probably have a lot of good ideas about how to solve problems with your loved one, but be sure that you listen to your partner's ideas too.
>
> ❧ If you have a discerning interpersonal style, you might tend to assume that your partner won't be responsive to your concerns. Try to give him or her a chance!
>
> ❧ If you have an open-minded interpersonal style, be aware of your potential to be aloof. Remember the interdependent nature of intimate relationships and how you need to help each other.

In this chapter you have seen that your romantic relationship poses special challenges, including sex-related differences. In the next chapter we will look at how compassionate assertiveness can be used with people to whom you have always been, and will always be, connected: your children and your parents. Instead of emphasizing gender, we will shift the focus to age. On one side are your parents, who raised you. On the other side are your children, whom you yourself are raising. Compassionate assertiveness can help you guide the younger generation and give proper respect to the older generation, without losing yourself in the process.

CHAPTER 11

Compassionate Assertiveness with Your Family

In the last chapter we looked at the special conditions of a couple's relationship, shining a spotlight on gender differences. In this chapter we will look at family relationships, with a focus on the people who raised you and those you are raising or have raised. Both sides of the parental coin involve commitment, responsibility, and love. And because of our primal connection to these people it can be very difficult to set appropriate boundaries, give support with no strings attached, or say no. Let's see how compassionate assertiveness can help.

Your Parents

Your biological parents gave you life. They (or in some cases, adoptive parents) raised you. They took care of your basic needs, instilled values, and guided you to make what in their minds were the right and proper choices. When you were growing up they also controlled your life to a large extent. They expected certain kinds of behavior from you, punished you when you violated important family rules, and guided you the best way they knew how. They probably had the best of intentions during those years, but undoubtedly they had their blind spots, baggage from their own growing-up years, and various other limitations.

Over the years, the balance of power has shifted. You are independent now, while your parents may be becoming more dependent on you as they age. They may not be as strong as they used to be, might not be able to drive anymore, or may need financial help on an occasional or regular basis—so now, to a degree, the roles are reversed.

In addition, as they age, your parents may be lonely and want more of your companionship and attention than they did previously, and if they don't get it they may feel neglected or ignored after all they did on your behalf when you were young. As a result, they might feel entitled to make demands on your time, which could put more pressure on you than you think is reasonable.

Your responses to your parents' needs and expectations are a result of complex causes and conditions. On the one hand, you may resist a feeling of responsibility towards them. After all, you have your own life to lead. You have a job, household responsibilities, and friends. In addition, you might struggle with emotional wounds or anger about the mistakes your parents made when you were growing up. Those memories might make it harder for you to feel generous and giving toward them.

On the other hand, you may not be able to meet all of your parents' expectations despite your best efforts. This may be the case even if you are grateful for all they have done for you, recognize that they did the best they could at the time, and appreciate the sacrifices they made on your behalf. If your parents are not satisfied with what you are able to do for them, that in turn could lead to anger, guilt, or frustration on your part.

How do you balance your needs with those of your parents? How can you develop the strength to respond to their requests without neglecting your own needs? You can begin by looking inward and contemplating the four basic principles of compassionate assertiveness:

1. Think about the causes and conditions that are influencing both you and your parents.

2. Acknowledge that what you do will have consequences for both you and your parents, and provide your children with a role model for how the elderly should be treated.

3. Be aware of your feelings and intentions. Do you want to be of help? If not, what is holding you back? If so, can you treat your parents the way you will want to be treated when you are their age?

4. Follow the middle way: Try to find a reasonable balance between their needs and yours, and let your parents know that you will do the best you can, but that you have your limits.

Focusing on these four principles will help you see the situation in a balanced way, forgive your parents for their limitations, and try to start fresh. You might also want to meditate on forgiveness if you have been withholding support because of resentment about the past. These principles will also help you recognize that we all try to do the best we can with the inner and outer resources we have at any given time.

As avenues of communication open up, it may be very helpful to learn more from your parents about their memories and the struggles they faced both as children and as parents. Ask them, "What was it like for you?" and listen to what they have to tell you. A client once told me, for instance, that his mother used to beat him as a child. Then one day my client asked her how she was disciplined as a child. She responded that her mother used to bite her as a form of discipline and that she had sworn she would never do that to her own children. Knowing what his mother had gone through as a child and seeing how much she had struggled to overcome her own childhood traumas gave my client a new perspective and helped him understand that his mother had made an effort to give her children better parenting than she herself had received.

Another way to cultivate an honest and caring relationship with your parents is to apologize for things you did when you were young that caused them pain. This, like other acts of humility and accountability, is hard for most of us to do. However, if you are able to apologize, or at least acknowledge the grief you caused your parents when you were younger ("I realize now that I gave you a few gray hairs when I was a teenager, and I'm sorry I was such a handful"), it may help them forgive you and free them to admit their own regrets. In time, this open communication will allow you to be generous as well as to acknowledge your current limitations, which may include not being able to meet all of your parents' needs and wants.

If the process of using compassionate assertiveness with your parents is successful, they will appreciate your ability to give a little more, as well as accept your need to set limits in a kind manner, and your mutual love, acceptance, and respect will grow. As for your part, you may become more aware that someday you may well be in your parents' shoes. The next time you feel impatient with your parents because they forget things, are slow moving, or don't hear as well as they used to, project thirty years ahead when you might have the same problem. As you are increasingly able to appreciate and identify with your parents, also keep in mind that someday you will lose them. This will help you savor the time you have together and will pave the way for peace on both sides and for no regrets on yours. Not only that, you will be modeling kindness toward the older generation for your children to remember when you are old.

An Invitation: Build a Bridge of Empathy

Think about your parents and their needs. Are there ever times when it is hard for you to give of yourself or make sacrifices for them? If so, how much is this due to other expenses or obligations? How much is because you feel angry and resentful? How much is because you feel indifferent toward them? Now think about how you would like your children or others to treat you when you are old. Consider vowing to treat your parents as you would like to be treated when you are their age.

○ *Liz the Adult Child*

Liz was a middle-aged married professional who came to see me because she found it difficult to be assertive both with her mother and with her two children. Here I describe the work we did on her relationship with her mother; later in this chapter I will describe how we worked on her relationship with her children.

When Liz was growing up it seemed like her parents were always angry with her. Among other things, they criticized her for not helping out more and they didn't like her friends, so they greatly restricted her opportunities to go out with them. Liz's efforts to negotiate with her parents fell on deaf ears, which led her to feel great frustration and helplessness, and one of her greatest goals was to be as different from them as possible when she grew up.

When she reached adulthood, Liz got a good job, got married, had kids, and gave herself some space from her parents. Over the years, Liz gained perspective and began to get along better with them. When her father died, she stepped in, taking her mother, Alice, on weekly trips to the grocery store and out for lunch.

Although Alice had mellowed over the years, she retained a sharp tongue and a critical attitude, which triggered Liz's old feelings of resentment and helplessness. But as Liz learned about compassionate assertiveness, she slowly gained the strength and wisdom to stand up to her mother instead of avoiding her. Let's see how she did it:

Cultivating gratitude and patience. Liz began spending a few minutes each day meditating about her mother and focusing on all her mother had done for her over the years, including tutoring her, making sure she stayed out of trouble, and teaching her how to cook and to balance a checkbook. She thought about how spunky and even courageous her mother was, and how proud she was of her mother's ability to put herself through college and her involvement with the civil rights movement in the 1960s. She began to keep a daily gratitude journal, including her memories from her growing-up years, as well as the more recent experiences with her mother that she was grateful for.

Using mindfulness to rein in anger and fear. Although Alice voiced appreciation for their outings, she often criticized Liz's driving and the food at the restaurants they went to, and she always commented when Liz was even a few minutes late. Liz tried to ignore Alice's complaints, but the wounds from her mother's barbs were starting to fester. Aware of her growing negative feelings toward her mother, Liz decided to use compassionate assertiveness with Alice. But first she reminded herself that:

○ **Actions are the result of complex causes and conditions.** Liz made an effort not to take her mother's criticisms too personally. She remembered that her grandmother had always been very critical of Alice, that her mother had endured many financial hardships over the years, and that when her husband died Alice lost her best friend. Liz began to appreciate that Alice's negativity was probably affected by all these factors. It dawned on Liz that if she had all of her mother's baggage, maybe she would be irritable too.

o **Actions have consequences.** Liz was starting to resent her mother's critical behavior and dread their weekly outings. She knew that if she didn't say anything to Alice, she would eventually decrease the frequency of her visits or become unduly irritable with her.

o **Intentions matter, and follow the middle way.** Liz decided to talk with her mother with the intention of improving their relationship. She did not want to reject her or to become verbally aggressive, nor did she want to feel like a doormat. Addressing her concerns in a calm and affectionate way made sense to her.

Using communication and negotiation skills. The next time they went out to lunch, Liz began to tell her mother about her feelings. She told Alice that she loved her and wanted to be there for her but that it bothered her that she didn't feel more appreciated. Alice surprised Liz by listening respectfully. They moved into problem-solving mode, and then the conversation became playful. Liz asked her mother what she should do if Alice slipped into critical mode. Alice replied that Liz could hit her over the head with her purse or strap her to the roof of the car. Liz then asked if Alice thought she might be able to make some positive comments before making a negative one. Her spunky mom laughed and said, "Well, if I have to do that, it looks like I won't ever be able to say anything critical!"

On a more serious note, Alice admitted that at times she was depressed and lonely. She also said hesitatingly that it was difficult for her to get herself up and dressed in the morning on Saturdays but that she hadn't wanted to complain. "Your dad and I used to shop in the afternoon. Do you think we could change the time of our visits?" Liz replied that they could, and with a mischievous smile she playfully added, "Of course, I'll have to charge you double for afternoon services." Without skipping a beat, her mother replied, "Put it on my account." Liz said that given all that her mother had done for her, she had plenty of credit in her account to draw from.

They then talked about looking into some nearby community events that Alice could attend, and agreed that it would do her some good. At the end of the visit, Alice patted Liz's cheek and, with mock seriousness betrayed by a gleam in her eye, said, "You know, you're not such a bad daughter after all; I don't care what anyone says. Does that count as a positive?" At that point, Liz knew that they could talk with each other in an honest and respectful way, using sharp humor to take the sting out of uncomfortable topics. They had turned an important corner in their relationship.

An Invitation: Strive to Reduce Conflict between You and Your Parents

Think about a past conflict you had with your parents and ask yourself the following questions:

What causes and conditions led to each of our positions?

What were the consequences?

What were my intentions? What do I think theirs were?

When conflicts arise in the future, can I find a middle way and...

1. *draw on compassion, gratitude, loving-kindness, patience, and forgiveness?*

2. *look at the big picture?*

3. *be mindful of anger and fear without being swept away by them?*

4. *communicate and negotiate with my parents in a caring and reasonable manner?*

Your Children

If you are a member of the "sandwich" generation, then your involvement with your aging parents will be balanced by the joys and challenges of raising a family of your own. My mother's admonition that I would not appreciate my parents until I had children of my own did not ring true when I was a teenager, but it does now.

When you become a parent you are responsible for nurturing your children and preparing them as best you can for the challenges they will face when they grow up, just as your parents did for you. To a large extent your children's strengths and weaknesses, their successes and failures will be incubated under your roof. Of course, no human being can ultimately control or be responsible for another person, but being a parent is about as close as you can get.

And how do you guide your youngsters? Most importantly, parents model behavior that their children will be watching and taking in, so "do as I say, not as I do" usually falls on deaf ears. And in terms of behaviors that you do and do not reward, remember that there are many kinds of rewards: attention, praise, monetary rewards, privileges, and so on. Setting firm but reasonable limits and encouraging communication and opportunities for negotiation are the hallmarks of parents who take their responsibilities to heart so that their children can develop to their highest potential. Most of all, there's love—that profound experience of deep and abiding commitment, driven by a multitude of causes and conditions, that makes you want to be the best you can be, not just for yourself, but for your child as well.

○ *Liz the Parent*

As Liz forged a healthier relationship with her mother, she also asked me for help dealing with her two children. Matt, age twelve, was a sweet boy, but was somewhat disorganized and irresponsible. Preferring video or computer games over schoolwork, he had to be continually reminded to do his assignments. Seven-year-old Sara was a social butterfly who worked hard in school for her teacher's and parents' approval, but she was also moody at times and prone to cry at the drop of a hat. Liz felt ineffective in motivating her kids to help around the house and worried about Matt's poor study habits and Sara's thin skin.

Some of Liz's difficulties had to do with her own assertiveness problems. Others had to do with the normal challenges of raising a family. Both Liz and her husband, Ron, worked long hours. Like many others in their situation, they often found themselves torn between important job-related events and their children's soccer games or parent–teacher conferences. Because they wanted to spend as much quality time as possible with their children, they hired others to clean their house and mow their lawn, which Liz worried could lead their children to think that household tasks were only done by hired help.

To avoid being overly authoritarian and to compensate for their limited time with their children, Liz and Ron avoided setting limits with them so as not to tarnish their time together with arguments. In addition, they had a hard time resisting Matt's relentless lobbying for his own cell phone, his own computer, a TV in his bedroom, and those popular but very expensive athletic shoes. Sara seemed unable to play by herself and pressured Liz to play dolls with her (Liz's least favorite activity) several times a week, and every weekend she wanted to invite a continuous stream of friends over, even though she would often get overtired and end up in tears.

Many people who come to me for help with parenting have similar problems. And single-parent families have the stress of added financial concerns and complicated visitation schedules to juggle, not to mention the weirdness of getting ready for a date while your child is doing the same.

At times the parents who seek consultation with me are more focused on their children's happiness, popularity, self-esteem, and academic success than on their learning responsibility, life skills, and empathy toward others. They are often surprised to learn that the more responsible, competent, and empathic their children are, the more likely they are to grow into the happy, confident, and successful adults their parents want them to be.

How can you give your child the benefits of today's vast opportunities while fostering the development of skills, attitudes, and values that will be most helpful as he or she moves through the childhood and teenage years?

A compassionate assertiveness perspective can help prepare you for the task. Let's use Liz and Ron's situation as an example:

○ **Actions are the result of complex causes and conditions.** The most important way to teach your values to your children is to model them yourself. If you want your child to be patient, model patience. If you want your child to be respectful, model respect toward others. I encouraged Liz and Ron to be attentive to this most valuable form of learning, and they worked hard to increase their awareness of this issue and change some of their own problematic habits, such as yelling at each other and gossiping about others.

Beyond modeling, create a climate of a team effort at home. Involve your children in cooking, cleaning, yard work, and other tasks that benefit the family. Support independence by celebrating your child's attempts, even if the outcome isn't perfect. Hard work, not success per se, should be your emphasis (although the latter is usually the outcome of the former). When our own children were growing up, my husband often intoned the old saying "The harder you work the luckier you get." It's a good one to remember.

○ **Actions have consequences.** As a parent you have more power than you may realize. Children love attention from their parents and will work very hard to get it. You can capitalize on this by giving your children lots of positive attention for behaving in ways consistent with your values. In addition, a smile and polite words, such as "Do you think you could…? I would really appreciate it" and "Thank you so much for…," can be very reinforcing. To guide you, try thinking about how you would have liked your parents to speak to you when you were a child.

Not surprisingly, when Liz and Ron showed appreciation to Matt and Sara for helping out, it made the children want to help out even more. Liz and Ron made it a point to compliment Matt when he followed parental instructions ("Thanks for taking your laundry downstairs when I asked you to—it really makes the job so much easier") and praising Sara when she was able to accept disappointment without crying ("I noticed that you were able to be flexible when we had to postpone going to the movies—thank you, honey"). Matt and Sara began to build their confidence and self-esteem by contributing to the welfare of the family, taking pride in a job well done, and practicing patience and self-discipline.

Another technique for motivating children is to establish an allowance system. Over many years of providing guidance to parents, I have found that a well-developed allowance system is one of the most powerful tools parents can use to teach their children some of life's most important skills—such as budgeting, which includes planning, making choices, and learning how to defer gratification, not to mention finding out why learning math matters. In addition, allowances paid for their contributions to the family give children confidence and good work habits. When a child learns how to put dishes in the dishwasher, dust furniture, or vacuum a floor, he is developing competence and a helpful attitude that his parents will appreciate and that will come in handy when he grows up (his or her spouse will thank you!).

I usually recommend that parents give their children a very small allowance just for being a member of the family but award additional money for doing chores and for demonstrating behaviors that illustrate flexibility, independence, and maturity, such as accepting no for an answer. Ron and Liz took my advice when I recommended that they be generous with allowances but stingy with giving "handouts" for cafeteria snacks or treats at the mall. This motivated Matt and Sara to earn more so they could have more to spend.

The parents included a rule that their children had to save half of their allowance for major purchases (or just for savings' sake) and put ten percent toward charity, making sure that the allowance was generous enough so that what was left over after this was enough for small purchases each week or for saving toward a larger purchase. To reinforce initiative, independence, and responsibility, the children received bonuses for fulfilling their obligations without being reminded. A chore chart posted on the refrigerator was a good visual reminder and kept things organized.

Because of their age difference, Matt received a larger allowance (potentially $22 per week, $10 in spending money after $10 went to savings and $2 to charity) for doing several chores, including putting in homework and study time. Seven-year-old Sara received a smaller allowance (up to $12 per week, of which $6 went to savings and $1.20 to charity, leaving her almost $5 per week for spending money). She had only a few chores, but her parents also included such behaviors as demonstrating patience and flexibility. This might sound like a lot of money, but it turned out to be only a little more than Liz and Ron had spent on the children prior to the allowance system. If you want to set up an allowance system, first keep track of how much you actually spend on your children in the course of a week or two so that you will have a benchmark.

And just as Matt and Sara received a small allowance for being members of the family, they were expected to help out when asked, even if the request was not an official chore. This was designed to prevent the children from thinking they had to get paid for everything they did.

The final tool that I'll mention is called the Premack principle, a technique that makes the activity the child wants to engage in (such as going on the Internet) contingent on doing what she needs to do first (for example, loading the dishwasher). Liz and Ron used this in tandem with the allowance system so that the kids wouldn't blow off parental requests or their chores, figuring that they didn't care that much about the money or privileges. Using the Premack principle, certain chores had to be completed or requests fulfilled before the children could watch TV, use the computer, or arrange a playdate.

○ **Intentions matter, and follow the middle way.** Ron and Liz set up the allowance system, giving the children input regarding their chores. They set up weekly family meetings to discuss the system, make modifications when needed, and distribute the allowances. They made every effort to practice (and model) good communication and negotiation skills. They made their intentions about the allowance system clear: it was set up because they loved their children and felt responsible for teaching them values, attitudes, and skills that would serve them well now and in the future. The parents used a reasonable and fair approach and maintained a positive attitude, which was transmitted to their children, who improved significantly in all areas of concern.

The techniques Liz and Ron used illustrate a compassionate assertiveness approach, one that supported and encouraged their children as well as helping them grow in ways that increased independence, responsibility, and initiative. With your newly acquired understanding and compassionate assertiveness skills, you can do the same. If you are interested in reading more about similar approaches to child-rearing, I highly recommend *Living with Children* (Patterson 1977) and *The Blessing of a Skinned Knee*, written from a Jewish perspective, but relevant for all families (Mogel 2001).

Consider the Implications for Your Interpersonal Style

- If you tend to have an enthusiastic interpersonal style, you may be very "into" trying these ideas with your parents or children. But be sure to listen to their perspective as well.

- If you have a discerning interpersonal style, remember to present your concerns and ideas in a way that communicates caring. Of course you should share your feelings, but avoid using a blaming tone when possible.

- If you have an open-minded interpersonal style, you might need to put extra effort into thinking things through so you can present your concerns, requests, or expectations to your parents or your children in a clear and well-thought-out manner.

In this chapter and the previous one we have looked at some of your closest relationships—those with your romantic partner, your parents, and your children. In the next and final chapter, you will learn how to apply compassionate assertiveness with those you encounter outside your inner circle of loved ones. This includes friends and people at work, in your community, and in the world beyond.

CHAPTER 12

Compassionate Assertiveness in the Outside World

We have looked at how you can use the principles and skills of compassionate assertiveness with your "inner circle" relationships: your spouse or partner, as well as your children and parents. In these relationships you have a commitment, a personal history, and a deep attachment. You care very much about these people and they are a big part of your life.

But what about people with whom you may not have these very deep connections, such as your extended family, friends, people at work, acquaintances, and strangers? There is a whole big world out there where compassionate assertiveness can be helpful as well. In this chapter we will explore how to use it to address the inevitable stresses and conflicts that you will need to face from time to time in life beyond your front gate.

The Buddhist Perspective: We're All Brothers and Sisters

Buddhism recognizes that we all have the tendency to prefer some people to others and to treat people preferentially in accordance with our relationship to them. It is natural for us to value and care about "my" mother, "my" boyfriend, and "my" child more than we care about others because of our self-centered "my." But Buddhist philosophy puts forth this challenge to consider: if you can put your ego on the back burner and tune in to your profound connections with others, you will be happier and more content. The Buddhist concepts that follow—"not so separate," "just like me," "you are special, just like everyone else," "sympathetic joy," and "loving-kindness"—are anti-ego positions. They provide special lessons for compassionate assertiveness with the outside world and for life in general. I hope they will be as useful to you as they have been to me. As you read, keep in mind that you can apply the four foundational principles of compassionate assertiveness to each topic: (1) actions are the result of complex causes and conditions, (2) actions have consequences, (3) intentions matter, and (4) follow the middle way.

Not So Separate

As discussed in earlier chapters, according to Buddhist philosophy we all suffer from negative emotions and unhealthy mental states. One such mental state is the illusion that we are separate and independent from others, especially those with whom we do not identify or have a close personal bond. This creates a wall between "us" and "them," which can reinforce fear, prejudice, or even hatred.

Buddhism asks you to recognize your connection with, and your effect on, everyone you encounter each day. This recognition will help you expand your circle of identification and soften your sense of separateness. Of course, this is easier said than done, especially when someone does something that leads you to feel afraid, hurt, or angry. But the good news is now that you have some training in compassionate assertiveness, you might be just a little bit better able to accomplish this. In the pages that follow, you will see how the lessons from the previous chapters—compassion, gratitude, patience, equanimity, forgiveness, mindfulness, caring communication, and skillful negotiation—can help you let go of your ego so you can bridge the gap between yourself and others and think of them as your "brothers" and "sisters."

Just Like Me

It is tempting to judge friends, people at work, those you encounter in the community, or people you read or hear about for things they have done that you disapprove of. But when people have done something you think is wrong, try to acknowledge that you cannot know all of the causes and conditions that led them to this behavior. Ask yourself, "If I had the exact same life experiences and was in the exact same situation, am I so sure I'd do much better?" Or even, "Have I ever done something similar in my life? Am I really so different from that person? Maybe, just like me, she has ups and downs, strengths and weaknesses, and good days and bad days" (Chodron 2007). The American novelist Willa Cather articulated this sentiment when she commented, "Sometimes a neighbor whom we have disliked [for] a lifetime for his arrogance and conceit lets fall a single commonplace remark that shows us another side, another man, really; a man uncertain, and puzzled, and in the dark like ourselves" (Cather 1931, 686).

You Are Special, Just Like Everyone Else

The Buddhist concept of "nothing special" is an important way of freeing us from thinking we are "better" or "worse" than others. The idea is that every person has the same potential for doing good or ill. Favorable conditions and circumstances can help inner goodness flourish, while unfavorable conditions can make it more difficult to be our best.

This perspective goes against the grain of our individualistic, competitive society, and it is very hard to diverge from what you may have been taught your whole life. But you do pay a price when you measure your worth by how you stack up against others.

Let's say, for instance, that because of your talents or life circumstances, you believe you are better than some other people. This attitude can lead to arrogance and self-centeredness. In turn, you can become filled with selfish pride and so focused on yourself that you forget you are basically not so different from all those people you interact with every day. They have flaws, just like you do, but they also may have many wonderful qualities you will never know about.

Alternatively, you may feel you are inferior to certain people and less worthy of care, kindness, or respect than they are, and you may even experience self-hatred or self-loathing. But this attitude is just as unhealthy as arrogance, because it can cut you off from your human connection with others and make you forget that, just like everyone else, you have inner goodness and are a lovable and worthwhile human being. Furthermore, if others sense your self-loathing, they may treat you as unworthy of love and respect. And that is not good for you—or for them.

Either extreme—arrogance or self-hatred—violates one of the fundamental Buddhist principles of compassionate assertiveness: while there is always work to be done, all of us are "nobly born" and deserve to be treated with kindness and compassion.

See what it feels like to think of yourself as "nothing special" and to experience yourself as connected to—not that different from and neither better nor worse than—others. Holding both humility and self-caring in your heart is not easy, but it will free you from having to constantly compare yourself to others. The Dalai Lama refers to himself as a simple monk who is nothing special (Dalai Lama 2005). If it works for him, I think it can work for the rest of us, too.

Sympathetic Joy

Another Buddhist concept important in dealing with people outside of your inner circle is sympathetic joy, which involves acknowledging our own positive qualities and enjoying our good fortune, and rejoicing in the positive qualities and good fortune of others as well. Sympathetic joy, then, means identifying with others, being happy with what we have, and letting go of jealousy and envy. And when we do feel sympathetic joy, it is important to express it as well. When your friend buys a new car or your coworker gets promoted, it is sympathetic joy that helps you offer heartfelt congratulations—"I'm so thrilled for you. Tell me more!"—instead of a jealous response like "Your new car's gas mileage isn't very good" or "That's going to be a nightmare of a job."

However, sympathetic joy doesn't apply only to people you may envy. It can also keep you from feeling pity or superiority toward people who have less than you. They have times of joy and peace, just as you do. In fact, many people who have very little from a material standpoint or have suffered hardships might be more content and happier than you in some ways. They may have more gratitude for what they do have, show more care toward others, or have skills and talents that you don't. Or maybe they have a higher level of self-discipline or a stronger spiritual life or are more in tune with nature. Therefore, even though I hope that your compassion, loving-kindness, and feelings of responsibility lead you to help those in need as best you can, there is no need to pity them, because that reflects an attitude of superiority that doesn't help you or them.

Loving-Kindness

Loving-kindness has been mentioned periodically throughout this book, but I would like to discuss it in more detail here. Loving-kindness is a close relative of sympathetic joy. While sympathetic joy celebrates the positive qualities, and good fortunes of others in the past or present, loving-kindness emphasizes wishing others good fortune and well-being in the future with unconditional friendliness and benevolence. At its highest level, loving-kindness means that you wish happiness for all beings without discrimination (Dalai Lama 2005).

This can be a hard concept for Westerners, with our individualistic values, to accept. But see if you can make an attempt to stretch your ideas about who is worthy of loving-kindness. Is it possible you can extend that warmhearted attitude to more and more people, maybe even those you don't like?

As an exercise, the next time you are walking down the street, see if you can extend thoughts of loving-kindness even to strangers, and whether you can extend the same degree of friendliness and consideration to an unattractive person in dirty clothes as to a person who is beautiful and well dressed. Remember that there are many conditions that caused you, and each of those two individuals, to hold this particular status in life at this moment. Like life itself, our circumstances continuously change, so try to cultivate and engage in whatever acts of loving-kindness you can, for as many others as you can, for as long as you can.

Loving-kindness, sympathetic joy, compassion, and equanimity constitute the "four immeasurables" or "four radiant abodes," which the Buddha entreated his monks to cultivate as antidotes to suffering (Kornfield 2008, 385–402). Contemplating the four immeasurables is an excellent way to create a foundation of goodwill between yourself and others, irrespective of your personal relationship with them.

For the remainder of this chapter, let's see how one woman applied the concepts above and used compassionate assertiveness in three settings in the outside world.

○ *JoAnn's Story*

JoAnn was a research assistant to the division chief at a large government agency. She came to see me because of anxiety and assertiveness problems she struggled with in numerous settings, including in the community, with friends, and at work.

In asking about her history, I learned that when she was growing up, JoAnn's father had a pattern of flying into rages, especially when JoAnn or her mother made even small requests. Her mother had never been able to protect JoAnn, or even herself, when her father was on the warpath, although she was very supportive of JoAnn when her father was not around. Both of her parents were now deceased.

As a result of her upbringing, JoAnn consistently avoided speaking up for fear of being criticized or of offending or alienating others. And because she was afraid to address concerns with others she often felt victimized, which led her at times to have a negative or bitter attitude toward the world.

As JoAnn learned and practiced compassionate assertiveness she began to feel more confidence in herself. She was able to see that her father's rages were symptoms of causes and conditions she would never fully understand. She now understood that she had suffered because of his temper and that although she had had to live with his problems as a child, she didn't have to let his issues cripple her now that she was an adult. Slowly JoAnn began to forgive her father. She was also able to forgive her mother, recognizing that she did not intend to leave JoAnn in harm's way but felt trapped and helpless due to her own limitations. This experience taught her that it is never too late to forgive, even after someone has died.

At the same time, JoAnn began to work on her extreme fear of conflict. Slowly she was able to increase her ability to say no and make reasonable requests of others. Here are some situations where she successfully used compassionate assertiveness to cultivate self-respect and healthier interactions with people in the outside world.

Using Compassionate Assertiveness with a Salesman

One day JoAnn was shopping for a lamp at her local department store. A salesperson came up to her two or three times to ask if she needed more help or had made a selection. Feeling irritated, JoAnn thought about how in the past she might have either left the store in order to escape the discomfort or bought a lamp in order to avoid offending or angering the salesman. This time she decided to test her compassionate assertiveness skills.

Awareness of causes and conditions. JoAnn took a few slow breaths and recognized that the salesperson's financial stresses might have led him to pester and pressure her and that he didn't intend to be obnoxious. She wondered what it would be like for her if she had his job and had to depend on commissions to pay her bills. Thinking this way helped her soften her irritation toward him, and even to appreciate his efforts to assist her.

Actions have consequences. JoAnn realized that if she left the store or made a purchase under these circumstances it would work against her goal of being more assertive. Furthermore, if she bought a lamp, it would likely harm the salesman, because he would be rewarded for being pushy. Being pushy wasn't good for him in general and could cause him to lose sales in the future or get him in trouble with his supervisor if someone complained about him.

Intentions matter. When the salesman approached her again a few minutes later, she smiled at him and said, "I know that you are trying to make a sale, and that your intention is to be a good salesperson, but I am feeling pressured. I don't want to feel that I have to make a purchase at this time."

Using caring communication/effective negotiations. She followed up with "I'd like to be left alone to browse. But if I decide to buy a lamp today or in the future when you are here, I'll seek you out. Do you have a business card?" He did, and he gave it to her. She thanked him and said, "I'll let you know when I'm ready to buy. How does that sound?" With a relieved smile, he agreed, and he kept his word. So did she.

Using Compassionate Assertiveness with a Friend

JoAnn's friend Monique had a habit of giving her unsolicited advice and then getting annoyed if JoAnn didn't take it. In these situations, JoAnn felt put on the spot, but in the past she hadn't said anything to Monique for fear of offending her. However, JoAnn now realized that it did not help their relationship for her to feel defensive or obligated to take Monique's advice.

One day JoAnn and Monique were talking about summer vacations. JoAnn said she was planning to go to a beach in Rhode Island. Monique responded that she had been there once and didn't really like it. She said she thought JoAnn would enjoy one of the Delaware beaches more. JoAnn, who had pretty much made up her mind, thanked her for her advice and they moved on to another subject. The next day Monique e-mailed her a number of links about the Delaware beaches and to the websites of several hotels there. JoAnn felt a little pressured by this. She sent Monique an e-mail thanking her for her effort but saying that she would probably stick to her original plan. She anticipated that Monique might bring the topic up again and decided that she'd better be ready.

In preparation, JoAnn spent some time contemplating gratitude by being mindful of how much she really liked Monique, who was a generous and funny person and a lot of fun to be with. She would keep that in mind to maintain her positive feelings toward Monique if she needed to speak up.

Sure enough, when they got together the following week to go bike riding, Monique asked if JoAnn had looked into the hotels she had e-mailed her about. JoAnn felt herself tensing up, took a few slow deep breaths, and decided to say something.

JoAnn: *(engaging in caring conversation)* "It was really sweet of you to take the time to send me those links, but I've decided to go to Rhode Island this year. Maybe I'll try Delaware some other year."

Monique: "Really? I can't believe you want to go to a place where the water doesn't even warm up until August!"

JoAnn: "I hope you're not hurt or angry that I'm not taking your advice."

Monique: "Of course not. If you want to go to Rhode Island I hope you have a good time. I was just trying to help."

JoAnn: *(intentions matter)* "I know you were. It's just that I don't want you to feel like you have to make sure that I make what you think is the best decision, so I hereby absolve you from that responsibility, now and in the future. And if I don't like Rhode Island, I promise I'll remind you that you told me so."

Monique: "Okay, I get the message. From now on, as long as you're all right with my sending you links I think you might like from time to time, I'll try not to convince you of my wisdom."

JoAnn: *(using humor)* "I already know you're wise. After all, you picked me to be your friend. I just hope you'll forgive me if I end up having a good time in Rhode Island."

Monique: "Yeah, yeah. Now how about going on that bike ride?"

Using Compassionate Assertiveness at Work

One day during a group meeting, JoAnn's boss, Margaret, criticized a report JoAnn had just written. JoAnn felt humiliated and angry. Not only was her report not appreciated, but for Margaret to lay into her in front of the others made things much worse. In the past, JoAnn would not have discussed her feelings for fear that Margaret would get upset or angry. But she had learned that using compassionate assertiveness could help in other situations, so she decided to use it here as well.

Meditating on sensations, thoughts, and positive emotions. That night JoAnn meditated on what had happened. She became mindful of her heart pounding and her stomach being in knots. She used slow, deep breaths to calm down and think more clearly. She brought to her awareness her gratitude for all the things she appreciated and admired about Margaret: she was friendly and dynamic, had taught JoAnn a lot, and was hardworking and very competent. Although Margaret had criticized JoAnn in public once before, JoAnn recognized that this was a rare event. These thoughts helped JoAnn soften her feelings toward Margaret and see the bigger picture.

JoAnn also got in touch with her emotions. She allowed herself to be aware of her anger and hurt. Looking deeper, she realized that she was worried she had lost status among her peers because of Margaret's criticism. While that was possible, rather than assume she could not face her coworkers the next day, she considered that the other people in the room knew she was a very good worker and very likely thought Margaret was out of line. They might also have identified and sympathized with JoAnn, since something like that might have happened to them in the past or could happen in the future. This helped her not assume that her coworkers now thought less of her.

Considering the four principles of compassionate assertiveness. JoAnn considered that causes and conditions she was not aware of might have contributed to Margaret's behavior. Maybe Margaret was under some personal stress or there was a problem at their company that JoAnn didn't know about. JoAnn realized that there would be negative consequences for her and her boss, and their relationship, if she did not say anything. JoAnn then got in touch with her intention, which was to resolve the problem in a friendly manner. Since Margaret was her superior, this was not a relationship between equals, so she would need to be sure to convey respect. But because her feelings had softened, she realized this would not be difficult. JoAnn would choose the middle way. She would not let anger get the best of her when she talked to Margaret; neither would she cry in front of Margaret or allow herself to chicken out altogether.

Engaging in caring communication. The next morning JoAnn called Margaret and asked if they could talk for a few minutes. Margaret agreed. JoAnn took a few deep breaths and went to Margaret's office, the report in hand. Sitting down, she began: "I wanted to check in with you about a few things. First, I'm so sorry that you didn't like my report. I want to go over it with you so I can find out what the problems are and fix them."

Margaret: "That's fine. Do you have it with you?"

JoAnn: *(assessing Margaret's intentions)* "I do. But before we go over it together I'd like to talk with you about yesterday. This is hard for me to bring up, but it will keep bothering me unless I do. So, anyway, I'm wondering if you had intended to criticize me in front of the group."

Margaret: "Actually, no. But I had a lot going on and wanted to be sure that the report was revised as soon as possible because I'm on a very tight deadline."

JoAnn: *(calmly expressing her concerns and noting that this is an exception)* "I can see why you felt pressured to say something. But I have to tell you that I was really embarrassed. It's unlike you to do something like that."

Margaret: "I'm sorry. I guess it just came out because it was on my mind, and I was upset."

JoAnn: *(speaking respectfully)* "I appreciate your apology. You know I want to produce the very highest quality work, and I'll give it my immediate attention and get it to you as soon as possible. I just ask that in the future you talk to me in private."

Margaret: "That's fair; and I'll try not to do it again."

JoAnn: "Thanks, Margaret. That means a lot to me. Shall we go over the report now or set up a time for later today?"

Moving Forward

In these three examples, JoAnn used compassionate assertiveness to resolve a potentially difficult interpersonal situation in a caring way. She kept her dignity without other people losing theirs, and she was pleased that the disastrous consequences she might have anticipated in the past did not occur. She realized that speaking up could have made the problems escalate, but she felt confident enough in her ability to handle the situation that she was willing to take the chance.

As she continued to practice compassionate assertiveness in a variety of situations, JoAnn became more comfortable using it. She was especially pleased that the approach was consistent with her values of not hurting other people's feelings. Over time, she discovered that when she was friendly and reasonable, most other people were as well. She used awareness of her interconnections with others to help her be assertive in a caring way that people were likely to respond to positively, but she knew that if they didn't she could take it in stride. She now realized that speaking up did not mean doing harm and that it was much better than always feeling like a victim. These understandings helped her trust herself and others in a way she had never before been able to.

An Invitation: Contemplate Connections

Take a few minutes to contemplate your connection with others—not only your partner, parents, and children, with whom bonds run deep and strong, but also all the people who have touched your life: friends and acquaintances, people at work and in your neighborhood. Now consider people you don't know, perhaps strangers you see on the street. See if you can expand the feeling of connection to the homeless person you walk past and the rich person in the limousine that drives by. They are not that different from you: we all have strengths, hopes, flaws, and fears. Imagine treating everyone with kindness, while having the inner strength to speak up in a respectful and caring way when necessary.

Consider the Implications for Your Interpersonal Style

- ❧ If you have enthusiastic tendencies, cultivate letting go. Let awareness of your connections with others help you override the temptations of greed or jealousy when you are in difficult situations with acquaintances, friends, coworkers, or people in the larger community.

- ❧ If you have discerning tendencies, use your inner wisdom to cultivate loving-kindness toward others so you can override anger or judgments when difficult moments come up as you interact with others in the outside world.

- ❧ If you have an open-minded and peaceful temperament, cultivate equanimity so you can resist any temptation to be indifferent toward those who are not in your inner circle.

As you have seen in this final chapter, the benefits of compassionate assertiveness can serve you far beyond your relationships with those who are near and dear to you. I hope that at this point you agree that speaking up in a caring way when needed not only helps you, but also helps everyone around you—from your dearest loved ones to strangers. Have the courage to do this and watch your life blossom.

Afterword

I hope the lessons in this guide have helped you begin to apply compassionate assertiveness to your relationships with your partner, family, friends, coworkers, and others. Perhaps you have also started looking for ways to use it with strangers and even with people you don't like. If so, compassionate assertiveness has helped you think in a different way about events that in the past might have led you to be aggressive with others or to condemn, judge, or ridicule them.

You may have noticed that these changes are not easy to make; the practice of compassionate assertiveness requires that you soften unpleasant feelings and attitudes as they bubble up into your conscious awareness. Your efforts have taken honesty and courage as you have worked not to be swept away by negative patterns of thoughts, emotions, and actions. Of course we all share these challenges, but your newly acquired knowledge and skills should help you find the strength to face them and work with them. Moving forward, it will be helpful to memorize the four key principles and to let them guide you when problems arise: (1) actions are the result of complex causes and conditions, (2) actions have consequences, (3) intentions matter, and (4) seek the middle way.

The compassionate assertiveness journey you have begun involves cultivating inner strength, personal growth, and the ability to retrain your mind. As you review and practice the skills in this book, try to be as patient and forgiving with yourself as you try to be toward others. Expect to stumble and even at times to fail as you fall back into some of your old patterns or when you are not successful through no fault of your own. When these setbacks occur, remember that the work you are doing with compassionate assertiveness involves venturing into uncharted territory. Whether you are successful or not at any given moment, if you practice your new skills and attitudes with diligence you will continue to move forward.

Finally, remember why you picked up this book in the first place. Maybe you held back from discussing problems or asserting yourself because you were afraid others would be hurt or angry or that they would reject you or retaliate. But most likely this led you to feel resentful or helpless. And since feelings have a way of "leaking" out, they may have been expressed through displaced anger, manipulation, avoidance, passive resistance, or physical symptoms. Now you know that you don't do anyone a favor when concerns are left to fester. You realize that you owe it to others (and to yourself) to address significant problems, make reasonable requests, and set limits when needed and that you can do so with a calm mind and an open heart. And you have a toolbox of knowledge and skills that will help you be assertive in a way that does not harm you or other people. Trust that the actions you take in the spirit of compassionate assertiveness will increase your happiness and well-being and that of others as well.

I would like to know what in this guide has worked for you and what has not. Please give me feedback through the compassionate assertiveness website (www.compassionateassertiveness.com) so that I can learn along with you, and together we can benefit others.

In closing, please accept my wishes and hopes for you:

May you be free from suffering and the causes of suffering.

May you find happiness and the causes of happiness.

May your heart be filled with compassion, loving-kindness, joy, and equanimity.

And may wisdom and peace be with you all the days of your life.

Resources

Print

Baer, Jean. 1976. *How to Be an Assertive (Not Aggressive) Woman in Life, in Love, and on the Job.* New York: New American Library.

Brantley, Jeffrey. 2007. *Calming Your Anxious Mind: How Mindfulness and Compassion Can Free You from Anxiety, Fear, and Panic.* 2nd ed. Oakland, CA: New Harbinger Publications.

Chodron, Pema. 2002. *The Places That Scare You: A Guide to Fearlessness in Difficult Times.* Boston: Shambhala.

———. 2006. *From Fear to Fearlessness* (CD). Boston: Shambhala Audio.

Ferrucci, Piero. 2006. *The Power of Kindness: The Unexpected Benefits of Leading a Compassionate Life.* New York: Jeremy P. Tarcher/Penguin.

Henepola Gunaratana, Bhante. 1996. *Mindfulness in Plain English: Revised and Expanded Edition.* Boston: Wisdom Publications.

Kabat-Zinn, Jon. 2005. *Wherever You Go, There You Are: Mindfulness Meditation in Everyday Life*, Tenth anniversary edition. New York: MJF Books.

Salzberg, Sharon. 2008. *The Kindness Handbook: A Practical Companion.* Boulder, CO: Sounds True.

Shambhala Sun magazine. shambhalasun.com.

Websites

American Association of Sexuality Educators, Counselors, and Therapists.
aasect.org.

Authentic Happiness (positive psychology website).
www.authentichappiness.sas.upenn.edu.

Insight Meditation Community of Washington.
imcw.org.

International Forgiveness Institute.
forgiveness-institute.org.

Interactive Questionnaires

The Five Love Languages.
www.5lovelanguages.com/assessments.

Gratitude Survey.
www.authentichappiness.sas.upenn.edu/questionnaires.aspx.

The Essential Difference: How Male or Female Is Your Brain? (empathy
quotient and systematizing quotient quizzes, based on Baron Cohen,
2003, 201–217).
www.guardian.co.uk/life/news/page/0,12983,937443,00.html.

References

Acton, John (Lord Acton). 1887. "Letter to Bishop Mandell Creighton." In *Bartlett's Familiar Quotations,* edited by Emily Morison Beck. Boston: Little, Brown, 1980.

Alan, Richard. 2006. *First Aid for the Betrayed: Recovering from the Devastation of an Affair; A Personal Guide to Healing.* Bloomington, IN: Trafford Publishing.

Alberti, Robert E., and Michael L. Emmons. 1970. *Your Perfect Right: Assertiveness and Equality in Your Life and Relationships.* 9th ed. Atascadero, CA: Impact Publishers.

Aune, Krystyna S., and Norman C. H. Wong. 2002. "Antecedents and Consequences of Adult Play in Romantic Relationships." *Personal Relationships* 9: 279–286. doi: 10.1111/1475–6811.00019.

Baron-Cohen, Simon. 2003. *The Essential Difference: Male and Female Brains and the Truth about Autism.* New York: Basic Books.

Batchelor, Stephen. 2009. *Buddhism without Beliefs: A Contemporary Guide to Awakening* (CD). Louisville, CO: Sounds True.

Beck, Aaron. 1976. *Cognitive Therapies and Emotional Disorders.* New York: New American Library.

Bloom, Paul. 2010. "The Moral Life of Babies." *New York Times,* May 5. http://www.nytimes.com/2010/05/09/magazine/09babies-t.html.

Bouchard, Thomas J., Jr., David T. Lykken, Matt McGue, Nancy L. Segal, and Auke Tellegen. 1990. "Sources of Human Psychological Differences: The Minnesota Study of Twins Reared Apart." *Science* 250: 223–228.

Bowen, Sarah, Katie Witkiewitz, Tiara Dillworth, Neha Chawla, Tracy Simpson, Brian Ustafin, Mary Larimer, Arthur Blume, George Parks, and Alan Marlett. 2006. "Mindfulness Meditation and Substance Use in an Incarcerated Population." *Psychology of Addictive Behaviors* 20: 343–347.

Boyce, Barry. 2010. "The Science of Love." *Shambhala Sun*, May, 45–98.

Brach, Tara. 2003. *Radical Acceptance: Embracing Your Life with the Heart of a Buddha*. New York: Bantam Dell.

Brizendine, Louann. 2006. *The Female Brain*. New York: Doubleday Broadway.

Burns, David D. 1999. *Feeling Good: The New Mood Therapy* (Rev. ed.). New York: HarperCollins.

Cather, Willa. 1931. *Shadows on the Rock* (epilogue). Lincoln: University of Nebraska Press (reprint, 2006).

Chapman, Gary. 1995. *The Five Love Languages: How to Express Heartfelt Commitment to Your Mate*. Chicago: Northfield/Moody.

Chesterton, G. K. 1986. *Orthodoxy (Collected Works,* Vol. 1). San Francisco: Ignatius Press.

———. 2001. *A Short History of England (Collected Works,* Vol. 20). San Francisco: Ignatius Press.

Chodron, Pema. 2007. *Don't Bite the Hook* (Audio CD). Boston: Shambhala Audio.

Cline, Austin. 2006. *Don't Believe Everything You Think: The 6 Basic Mistakes We Make in Thinking*. Amherst, NY: Prometheus Books.

Creswell, J. David, Baldwin M. Way, Naomi Eisenberger, and Matthew Lieberman. 2007. "Neural Correlates of Dispositional Mindfulness During Affect Labeling." *Psychosomatic Medicine* 69:560–565.

Dalai Lama (Tenzin Gyatso). 1997. *The Four Noble Truths* (CD). London: The Office of Tibet.

————. 2005. *Eight Verses for Training the Mind* (CD, Discs 1 and 4). Ithaca, NY: Snow Lion Publications.

Dossick, Wayne. 1995. *Living Judaism: The Complete Guide to Jewish Belief, Tradition, and Practice.* New York: HarperCollins.

Eliot, Lise. 2009. *Pink Brain, Blue Brain: How Small Differences Grow into Troublesome Gaps—and What We Can Do about It.* New York: Mariner Books.

Emmons, Robert A., and Michael E. McCullough. 2003. "Counting Blessings Versus Burdens: An Experimental Investigation of Gratitude and Subjective Well-Being in Daily Life." *Journal of Personality and Social Psychology* 84:377–389.

Enright, Robert. 2001. *Forgiveness Is a Choice.* Washington, DC: APA LifeTools.

Fisher, Roger, William Ury, and Bruce Patton. 1991. *Getting to Yes: Negotiating Agreement without Giving In.* New York: Penguin.

Flanagan, Owen, Jr. 2006. "The Bodhisattva's Brain: Neuroscience and Happiness." In *Buddhist Thought and Applied Psychological Research: Transcending the Boundaries,* edited by D. K. Navriyal, Michael S. Drummond, and Y. B. Lai, 149–175. New York: Routledge.

Gaertner, Johannes A. 1994. *Worldly Virtues: A Catalog of Reflections.* New York: Viking Adult.

Gladwell, Malcolm. 2005. *Blink: The Power of Thinking without Thinking.* New York: Little, Brown.

Hanson, Rick. 2009. *Buddha's Brain: The Practical Neuroscience of Happiness, Love, and Wisdom.* Oakland, CA: New Harbinger Publications.

Hayes, Steven C., Victoria M. Follette, and Marsha M. Linehan. 2011. *Mindfulness and Acceptance: Expanding the Cognitive-Behavioral Tradition.* New York: Guilford Press.

Hölzel, Britta K., James Carmody, Mark Vangel, Christina Congleton, Sita M. Yerramsetti, Tim Gard, and Sara W. Lazar. 2011. "Mindfulness Practice Leads to Increases in Regional Brain Gray Matter Density." *Psychiatry Research: Neuroimaging* 191: 36–43.

Jones, Warren, and Kathleen Lawler. 2001. *Assessment of Forgiveness: Psychometric, Interpersonal, and Psychophysiological Correlates.* Knoxville: University of Tennessee Press.

Kabat-Zinn, Jon. 1990. *Full Catastrophe Living: Using the Wisdom of Your Body and Mind to Face Stress, Pain, and Illness.* New York: Bantam Dell.

———. 2005. *Guided Mindfulness Meditation* (CD). Boulder, CO: Sounds True.

Katz, Michael, and Gershon Schwartz. 1997. *Swimming in the Sea of Talmud: Lessons for Everyday Living.* Philadelphia: Jewish Publication Society.

Kimura, Doreen. 1999. *Sex and Cognition.* Boston: MIT Press.

Kornfield, Jack. 2007. *Guided Meditation: Six Essential Practices to Cultivate Love, Awareness, and Wisdom.* Louisville, CO: Sounds True.

———. 2008. *The Wise Heart: A Guide to the Universal Teachings of Buddhist Psychology.* New York: Bantam Books.

Lazar, Sara W., Catherine E. Kerr, Rachel Wasserman, Jeremy Gray, Doug Greve, Michael Treadway, et al. 2005. "Meditation Experience Is Associated with Increased Cortical Thickness." *NeuroReport* 16: 1893–1897.

Luskin, Fred. 2002. *Forgive for Good: A Proven Prescription for Health and Happiness.* New York: HarperCollins.

Lutz, Antoine, Julie Brefczynski-Lewis, Tom Johnstone, and Richard Davidson. 2008. "Regulation of the Neural Circuitry of Emotion by Compassion Meditation: Effects of Meditative Expertise." *PLoS One* 3: e1897.

MacLean, Paul D. 1990. *The Triune Brain in Evolution: Role in Paleocerebral Functions.* New York: Springer.

Martin, Rod A. 2006. The Psychology of Humor: An Integrative Approach. London: Elsevier Academic Press.

Mayo Clinic. 2010. "Constant Stress Puts Your Health at Risk." http://www.mayoclinic.com/health/stress/SR00001.

McCullough, Michael E., Robert A. Emmons, and Jo-Ann Tsang. 2002. "The Grateful Disposition: A Conceptual and Empirical Topography." *Journal of Personality and Social Psychology* 82: 112–127.

McKay, Matthew, Martha Davis, and Patrick Fanning. 2009. *Messages: The Communication Skills Book*. 3rd ed. Oakland, CA: New Harbinger Publications.

Miller, Jeffrey. 2005. "The Golden Buddha at Wat Traimit." *Korean Times*, June 2.

Mogel, Wendy. 2001. *The Blessing of a Skinned Knee*. New York, Penguin Putnam Inc.

Nidich, Sanford I., Maxwell V. Rainforth, David A. F. Haaga, John Hagelin, John W. Salerno, Fred Travis, Melissa Tanner, Carolyn Gaylord-King, Sarina Grosswald, and Robert H. Schneider. 2009. "A Randomized Controlled Trial on Effects of Transcendental Meditation Program on Blood Pressure, Psychological Distress, and Coping in Young Adults." *American Journal of Hypertension* 22: 1326–1331.

Paterson, Randy J. 2000. *The Assertiveness Workbook: How to Express Your Ideas and Stand Up for Yourself at Work and in Relationships*. Oakland, CA: New Harbinger Publications.

Patterson, Gerald R. 1977. *Living with Children: New Methods for Parents and Teachers*. Champaign, IL: Research Press.

Pinker, Steven. 2002. "Gender." *The Blank Slate: The Modern Denial of Human Nature*, 337–371. New York: Penguin Books.

Rosenberg, Marshall. 2003. *Nonviolent Communication: A Language of Life*. 2nd ed. Encinitas, CA: PuddleDancer Press.

Salzberg, Sharon. 2011. *Real Happiness: The Power of Meditation: A 28-Day Program, with Audio Recording*. Boulder, CO: Sounds True.

Schmidt, Amita. 2009. "Which Personality Type Are You?" *Tricycle*, Spring. http://www.tricycle.com/feature/which-buddhist-personality -type-are-you.

Seligman, Martin. 2002. *Authentic Happiness: Using the New Positive Psychology to Realize Your Potential for Lasting Fulfillment.* New York: Free Press.

Shapiro, Rami, trans. 2006. *Pirke Avot: Ethics of the Sages Annotated and Explained (chap. 4, verse 1).* Woodstock, VT: Skylight Paths Publishing.

Slagter, Heleen A., Antoine Lutz, Lawrence Greischar, Andrew Francis, Sander Nieuwenhuis, James Davis, and Richard J. Davidson. 2007. "Mental Training Affects Distribution of Limited Brain Resources." *PLoS Biology* 5: e166.

Tabak, Benjamin A., Michael E. McCullough, Lindsey R. Luna, Giacomo Bono, and Jack W. Berry. 2012. "Conciliatory Gestures Facilitate Forgiveness and Feelings of Friendship by Making Transgressors Appear More Agreeable." *Journal of Personality.* doi:10.1111/j.1467 -6494.2011.00728.x.

Tannen, Deborah. 1990. *You Just Don't Understand: Women and Men In Conversation.* New York: Ballantine Books.

Taylor, Shelley E. 2000. "Biobehavioral Responses to Stress of Females: Tend and Befriend, Not Fight or Flight." *Psychological Review* 107: 411–429.

Thich Nhat Hanh. 1990. *Present Moment Wonderful Moment: Mindfulness Verses for Daily Living.* Berkeley, CA: Parallax Press.

Warneken, Felix, and Michael Tomasello. 2006. "Altruistic Helping in Human Infants and Young Chimpanzees." *Science* 311: 1301–1303.

Young, Shinzen. 2002. *The Beginner's Guide to Meditation* (CD). Louisville, CO: Sounds True.

Sherrie M. Vavrichek, LCSW-C, is a cognitive behavioral therapist and published author who uses mindfulness, meditation, and Buddhist philosophy in her practice and in her life. She is a senior staff member at the Behavior Therapy Center of Greater Washington, and has presented at national conferences on numerous mental health topics, including compassionate assertiveness. Vavrichek lives and works in the Washington, DC area.

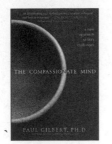
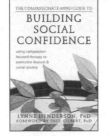

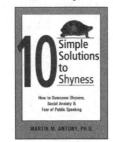